Savez-vous planter les choux?

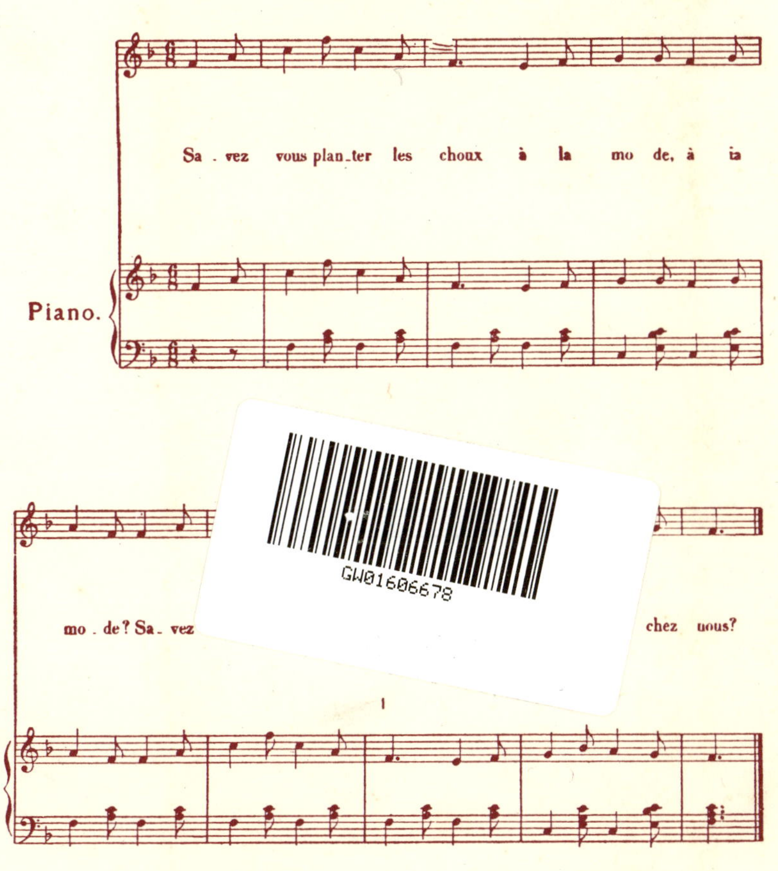

Savez-vous planter les choux?

A DAY
TO REMEMBER

A DAY
TO REMEMBER

Jerrard Tickell

I hear the voice you cannot hear,
   Which cries I must not stay;
I see a hand you cannot see,
   Which beckons me away.
            Thomas Tickell 1686–1740

KAYE & WARD
LONDON

First printed by Hodder & Stoughton 1952
under the title
The Hand and Flower
Reprinted by Kaye & Ward Ltd
21 New Street, London EC2M 4NT 1975

ISBN 0 7182 1105 7

Printed in Great Britain by
REDWOOD BURN LIMITED
Trowbridge & Esher

FOR

MY DEAR MOTHER

CHAPTER ONE

It was Saturday night in the public bar of The Hand and Flower.

The swing-doors stood open to the summer dusk of Saint John's Wood, the room was thick with smoke and a noisy game of darts was nearing its end. The score was one game all. Charley Brewer, local coalman and captain of the Darts Club, took a deep swig of mild ale, wiped his mouth and contemplated the scribbled chalk marks on the scoreboard. He pondered the mathematical problem laboriously.

"Ninety-one to get. That's eleven and two double tops. Order the beer, mate."

He threw his first dart unerringly into the eleven. The others crowded round. "Nice work, Charley boy. Keep it up." His next dart went into the double twenty. There was a roar of approval and men left their beer to watch the last, deciding throw. Conversation was stilled by the authoritative voice of Fred Collins, the landlord. "Silence, gentlemen, *please*. I must 'ave 'ush." Charley took his time. He hitched up the comfortable bulge of his trousers, sucked the tip of his dart and threw it. It hit the wire of the double twenty, quivered for a breathless second and fell to the floor. Charley used a wicked word. Emma Collins, the landlord's wife, said sharply:

"That's enough of that. Moderate your language, *please*. You're not in France *yet,* Charley. Tomorrow's time enough —when no one will understand you, anyway."

Charley Brewer bowed with exaggerated politeness.

"I beg your pardon, I'm sure. Roll on tomorrow."

The game and match went to Charley's opponents. Rounds of mild ale were ordered for the victors by the vanquished. As conversation became general, a man came unobtrusively into the bar. He was in his early thirties, and he had restless eyes that seemed to glance everywhere at once. He made his way to the counter and said softly:

"Small whisky, please."

As Mrs. Collins turned to serve the measure, she looked into the looking-glass and frowned. There was something familiar about this man's face and in the set of his shoulders.

She put the whisky on the counter and said archly, looking with a sidelong glance into his face:

"Soda?"

"Please."

She flipped the crown cork off a small bottle of soda, took his half-crown, threw it into the till, listening automatically for the jingle that would tell her that it wasn't counterfeit, gave him his change. As he took it carelessly, recognition came to her. She said, beaming:

"Bless me, if it isn't Mr. Hilgrove!"

He gave a slight start and then a reluctant grin.

"Yes, it's me all right. You all right, Mrs. Collins?"

"Oh yes, I'm lovely. You've been away, haven't you?"

He said shortly, "Yes. I've been away in the country."

"It's nice in the country, Mr. Hilgrove. Very nice. You back in London now?"

"Yes. I'm back in London now."

"Let me think. You've been away since . . . um . . . since last summer. Fancy that now! I've got an aunt in the country. I suppose you didn't meet her? Her name's Webb, Mrs. Sophy Webb, and she lives in the country. She's quite near Maidstone."

"No, I didn't meet her." He raised his glass. "Your good health, Mrs. Collins."

"Cheerio, Mr. H."

As Mrs. Collins turned again, Trevor Hilgrove looked carefully round the public bar. Nothing had changed during the year—or rather the eternity—that he had been in the country. He saw the pitted, pock-marked dart-board with the crude crest over it, two darts crossed over a tankard and the letters H. & F.D.C. above—Hand and Flower Darts Club. He saw the six wooden beer handles bound in shining brass; the glass case of dry sandwiches and meat-pies, the advertisement showcards for somebody's stout and the other showcard for somebody's cider, these with illustrations of the sort of languorous, pliant, wholly acquiescent women who came to disturb your dreams when you were—in the country. He saw the wet circles left by pint glasses on the counter, the scrubbed benches, the rows of twinkling bottles on the shelf behind.

From things to people.

Mrs. Collins was just the same, and the year that had marked him so grievously had not touched one of her kiss-curls or amplified her already ample bosom. He glanced at Charley Brewer, the coarse, Rabelaisian, kindly coalman, who bought and paid for cheese-rolls and soaked them in beer to give to his horse; he saw Mr. Grenfell and wondered, as he had so often wondered before, why the man to whom all doors were open should have chosen to cross the threshold of the public bar and to seek the society of those with whom he had so little in common. Luke Grenfell had been to a very expensive public school and up at Oxford. His clothes, conscientiously shabby, had once been very good clothes. It was hardly surprising that the regulars of The Hand and Flower should at first have regarded his deliberate intrusion into their sawdust kingdom with suspicion. They had looked for a sinister motive, but found none; anticipating patronage, they had only found humility; watchful against condescension, they had found sincerity and a rare delicacy in dealing. Gradually, over the months, he had been accepted in the role of eccentric, and his first nickname of "Little Lord Muck" had fallen into disuse.

But not by Shorty.

Shorty—who ran for Mr. McIsaac the bookie—had steadily refused to have anything to do with Mr. Grenfell. When Mr. Grenfell bought a round of drinks, Shorty always said swiftly, "Not for me. I can stand on my own two feet, thanking you." Trevor Hilgrove's glance shifted. There *was* Shorty, truculent as usual, more than a little ridiculous with his built-up shoulders and his shoes whose heels had an extra lift. If the Almighty made man in His Own Image, thought Trevor, He must have run out of raw material when He made Shorty. . . .

"Here we are again, Mr. Hilgrove. You in London for a bit now?"

"I expect so. But you never know. Here today—gone tomorrow. I'm a restless fellow."

He turned as a new-comer walked into the bar. This was a man of about twenty-eight, with a lean, rather solemn face. He carried himself with a calm assurance that Trevor found vaguely disquieting. He wore a tweed jacket, cut like a hacking coat, flannel trousers and a regimental tie. The recognition of symbols was part of Trevor's stock-in-trade, and he isolated the tie immediately. Army—Cavalry—Lancers—Tanks. That explained the square shoulders, the straight back and the easy effortless stride. Though a stranger to Trevor, he was obviously known and well-liked in the bar, for even the morose Shorty joined in the general chorus of "'Evening, Jim." He ordered half a pint of bitter and lit a cigarette. Trevor watched him covertly as he talked to Luke Grenfell. There was a curious reserve about him, a curious sense that he was in but not of the public bar of The Hand and Flower. Trevor Hilgrove disliked mysteries. As Mrs. Collins fluffed along the bar, he turned towards her, hunching his shoulders a little. He said with studied unconcern:

"Who's the chap in the sports coat and the Lancer tie, Mrs. Collins? I seem to know his face."

"Which one? Oh yes, I see. That's Jim Carver."

"Jim Carver. I think I've met him somewhere. What does he do?"

"He's in business, export business, I think it is. He's not really a London chap. Comes from the country, somewhere near Gloucester, I think. Used to be in the Army. A sergeant he was, and went through the whole war and got wounded in France towards the end. He's been funny, quiet like, ever since he got his demob. I didn't know he was in the Lancers. All soldiers are the same to me, except the Guards in their red coats and the Kilties. Jim's courting Cherry, you know; Cherry Mitchell, old Bill Mitchell the greengrocer's girl. Well . . . I say *he's* courting *her*, but if I was to have my say, it's the other way round. Still, least said soonest mended. Mr. Mitchell's a sidesman at Saint Saviour's and takes up the collection."

Trevor Hilgrove's voice was easy, but his eyes were as bright and as sharp as needles.

"The war changed a lot of us. How has he changed—Jim Carver, I mean, not the pious greengrocer?"

"Oh, I dunno. He hasn't been the same, not since he left the Army and took up with Cherry Mitchell. Chalk and cheese, that's what it is. Come to think of it, Mr. H., you're not looking too bright yourself. Been working indoors?"

Trevor Hilgrove gave a short laugh.

"That's right. I've been indoors too much. And the weather has been none too good where I was."

"It's beautiful now. The boys will have a lovely day tomorrow."

"What's on tomorrow?"

"Don't you know?" She tucked an errant curl back into the

golden halo from which it had wandered. "I would have presumed that everybody in the Wood knew all about tomorrow. It's the Darts Club Outing."

"Oh. Where are they off to? Margate?"

Mrs. Collins gave him a pulverising glance.

"Margate! I should think not, indeed. They're going to France."

Trevor Hilgrove stiffened. His mind, lazily reminiscing in this familiar place, suddenly became receptive and alive. He looked at Mrs. Collins with innocently raised eyebrows. He said softly:

"France, indeed. That's very interesting. Where to in France?"

"To Boolong."

"Where?"

"Boolong. You know, Boolong."

"Ah. Boulogne." His pronunciation was easy and accentless. Mrs. Collins said gamely, "That's what I said, 'Boolong.'"

"And how long are they going to Boulogne for?"

"Oh, just for the day. Meet here eight punctual, sharra to Victoria—Mr. Collins is putting on the beer for that little ride: two dozen lights, half a dozen Guinness and three of gin—train leaves at nine and the party gets to Boolong at a quarter-past twelve."

"Boulogne. That means they go *via* Folkestone."

"That's right, Mr. Hilgrove. Then Mr. Collins has arranged a nice middle-day dinner for them in Boolong, and they leave at a quarter-past six in the evening and get back at ten to Victoria, where the same sharra will be waiting to bring them back here."

"So they'll be in France for about six hours."

"That's right." She sniffed. "There are no ladies in the party, but only gentlemen; so I can't imagine what they'll get up to, I'm sure."

It was with an effort that Trevor Hilgrove kept his voice easy.

"Who are going?"

"Well, Jim Carver to begin with, and Charley, and Mr. Grenfell, the gentleman there in the corner with the horn-rimmed glasses. Four of my saloon bar customers are coming, and Shorty there, who runs for Mr. McIsaac, the bookie. Mr. Collins, I need hardly say, is Master of Ceremonies. Bert

Morgan was in the party, too, but he can't come now because of his Mum's varicose." She looked round haughtily at Charley Brewer, who was tapping impatiently on the bar with a shilling. "All right, Charley, all right. You still got half an hour. Pardon me, Mr. Hilgrove."

Mrs. Collins moved up the bar. Trevor Hilgrove lit a cigarette with fingers that trembled a little, drew so hard that the tip glowed redly. What extraordinary chance had sent him into The Hand and Flower on this of all evenings, what even more extraordinary chance had inflicted Bert Morgan's mother's legs with timely varicose? Once submerged in the society of these genial men, he would surely pass through Folkestone unnoticed—and beyond Folkestone lay France, and in France could lie fortune. Trevor Hilgrove was a man of quick decision. He caught Mrs. Collins's eye and smiled. She sailed up to him.

"That's better," she said, "that's more like the cheerful Mr. H. I used to know."

"Well, Mrs. Collins, what may I have the pleasure of ordering for you?"

"You're very kind, I'm sure. I'd like a small port."

"No you wouldn't, Mrs. Collins. You'd like a *large* port. And I'll take a large whisky this time. Well, again your good health. Now listen, Mrs. Collins. I could do with a bit of a holiday myself, and as Bert Morgan's dropped out, I see no reason why, provided the Darts Club has no objection, I shouldn't string along too. . . ."

CHAPTER TWO

JIM CARVER glanced at his watch, said a friendly "Good night" and left The Hand and Flower. He had an appointment with Cherry Mitchell at ten o'clock, and it wanted five minutes to the hour. He walked leisurely to where she lived with her widower father over the greengrocer's shop and rang the side-door bell, giving his own special ring that Cherry knew. As he heard her footsteps come running down the stairs, he smiled.

She opened the door. The hall light under its fringed shade shone behind her, illuminating the ordered corrugations of her fair hair so that it looked as if she had a halo. Her face was in darkness. She stood on tiptoe to receive his customary kiss. She said excitedly:

"It's come."

"What's come?"

"The thing for your friend. You know. It's lovely."

"I'd like to have a look at it."

"Of course, Jim. It's in the shop."

He followed her along the hall and into the shop by the back door. She switched on the light. It stood on the counter beside the till. Jim Carver looked at it for a long time without speaking. It was unbelievably hideous. He said at last:

"It's very nice."

"I'm ever so glad you like it. It's called 'The Broken Column', and Dad got it from a friend in the business—wholesale. It should have cost two pounds ten, but he got it on the nod for thirty shillings. I think it's lovely—and you see what's on the top. It's poetic—like Shakespeare."

"Yes, I see."

It wasn't a thing you could help seeing. It was the final touch, the one thing that gave the last comic twist to the already macabre. He said:

"I'll settle up straightway." He took out his wallet and gave her a pound note and a ten shilling note. She rang up the sum on the till, snapped the notes into their little clip, shut the drawer. She said, "I'll wrap it up for you, Jim. Dad's upstairs listening to the wireless, so I thought we'd go out for a walk." She paused. "I'd like to talk to you, Jim."

He wondered with a touch of disquiet what the subject of their conversation would be.

"Yes. Let's go out. It's a lovely night."

He watched her as she shrouded its ugliness in kindly, concealing sheets of brown paper. She had her back to him and, because of that, he had time to consider her almost academically. He had known her for a long time, over a year now. They had first met at the house of a friend of his from the office. He had been asked at the last moment because somebody had fallen out and, on being introduced, he had been aware of the veiled hostility of a disappointed girl who had expected someone else. As the evening had worn on, Cherry's initial coolness had warmed towards this simple and sincere man, and when he asked her if he might escort her home, she agreed with alacrity. By labyrinthine questioning she had found out that he was aged twenty-eight, a bachelor and doing very well in his firm. At the time she was reasonably unattached . . . and, in any case, he was a nice boy with grey eyes and strong, steady hands, not the pawing sort, but the nice steady sort. A girl might do a lot worse than Jim Carver, a lot worse.

That is how Cherry had seen Jim. How had Jim seen Cherry?

She was pretty, with a soft, blinking prettiness—and yet he had the feeling that Miss Cherry Mitchell knew exactly what she was at. Her kitten's eyes were remarkably shrewd, and her dress had been designed to emphasise her slim hips, her silken legs and her little high breasts. She gave him an impression of neatness, and that he liked. Her stockings fitted with never a wrinkle, her finger-nails were perfect and her fair hair had been waved with precision. He could visualise no situation from which she would not emerge looking as she did now, trim, fresh, self-possessed. He found her an attractive girl with no silly nonsense about her.

Walking to Saint John's Wood at his side she had not, as was her habit with young men, taken his arm. She had sensed that even the most remote physical contact would embarrass him at this early stage, and she had been right. Ignorant of the etiquette of the doorstep, Jim had speculated silently and furiously if the right thing to do was to kiss her good night. He had been much relieved when she had offered him her hand in a cool but friendly clasp. Nice girl. So nice a girl was she that he would have liked to see her again, but he didn't know the formula and the door had shut behind her before he found the right words. On the way home he had found excuses for his own lack of temerity by saying to himself that a girl like that must have dozens of boy-friends anyway, and that he had been wise not to risk a rebuff. Still, he would have liked to have seen her again.

Jim needn't have worried, for Cherry had no intention whatsoever of losing sight of this quiet, good-looking bachelor with the grey eyes and the steady job. She contrived that they should meet again very soon, before his first impression of her should have had time to fade. This time he had asked her if she would like to come to the pictures sometime, and Cherry had said that she would be ever so pleased. How about Saturday? Yes. Saturday would be lovely.

That visit to the pictures had been the first of many outings. It had been followed by excursions to Kew Gardens, to the Zoo, to Hampton Court, to Richmond by river steamer. Cherry took his arm nowadays as if by right, and she was practically always there when he rang up and suggested spending an evening together. Dad liked him, too. But Jim was obstinately uncommunicative about what she most wanted to hear—his plans for the future. She had become a habit and, realising it, took steps to make him conscious of the fact that she was not only a neat young lady in a navy costume but also a woman of flesh and blood. Coming home from the pictures one night last April, she had suggested walking the last bit of the way home—along a deserted road. As they had passed by the shell of a bombed house, she had said in her kittenish voice, "Let's explore." Within the dark and draughty walls, he had realised that this was clearly the time and place to kiss her and he had been startled by the warmth with which she had received his inexpert embrace. It was hard to reconcile the remote and self-possessed young lady who had sat beside him in the Odeon with the trembling girl who drew his face down to hers—while the moon made a tapestry of light through the broken slats and the wind swung a drunken door on its rusty hinge.

Now that the seed had been sown, Cherry had withdrawn

into herself. She had given Jim a slight foretaste of what he might expect—if and when. In spite of the return of her reserve, this was a different Cherry. There was about her a new determination, a new possessiveness, and more and more clearly did Jim come to know that theirs was an association from which only one end was expected of him. Nowadays they always kissed when they met and when they parted. They were the bread-and-butter kisses of people between whom there was an unspoken understanding, and most of the time Jim was well content. But sometimes in a high wind or hearing a phrase of music, his muscles would stiffen and his brow furrow in a bewildering desire for something that lay just beyond the reach of his imagination and of his hands.

He looked at her now and saw, through the transparent white blouse, the pale blue straps of her slip. He saw the slender hips, the unwrinkled stockings. He frowned. How little he knew of her really. For a brief moment in the bombed house she had made him aware that she possessed, under her neat, constricting garments, a breathless and pliant body. Having indicated its existence she had, as it were, returned it to store. But the message had been realised and, in a vague way, the episode had made Jim comfort himself with the rather muddled assurance that 'that sort of thing' would work out all right when the time came.

She tied up his parcel with practised dexterity, making a strong loop with the string. She turned round.

"There we are. That'll be nice and easy for you to carry. We can leave it in the hall and you can take it with you when we come back. I'll just pop upstairs and get a scarf."

He said, smiling affectionately, "Don't be long."

"I won't."

They walked slowly, arm-in-arm, aimlessly through the leafy roads of Saint John's Wood. For a long time neither of them spoke. Then Cherry said in a voice that was curiously timid and unlike her own:

"Jim, may I say something to you?"

"Of course, Cherry. What is it?"

"It's not an easy thing for me to say, Jim."

This was it. He tucked her arm more closely, more intimately into his. He said evenly, aware of what was coming:

"Go ahead."

"Well, it's only this—and it's not me, it's Dad. He's beginning to ask questions. We've been going about together now since long before last Christmas, and well, here we are still. I thought, we all thought, that when you got your rise in April you might say something, but somehow you didn't, and now it's July. You . . . you do want to settle down sometime, don't you, Jim?"

"Of course I do, Cherry. It's only . . . it's only . . ."

What was it? Jim frowned in the dusk. He was very fond of Cherry. Of course he was fond of her. They'd had a lot of good times together, over these last months—and it was quite true what she'd said—that he'd had an increase in salary in April. Suppose he did ask Cherry to marry him, they could be quite comfortable, living in London. They could even run to a small car—in London. But suppose a baby came along, it would be born in London, to breathe the burned petrol of London into its lungs, and the only air it would get would be the stale air of the streets. It wouldn't be born in the Cotswolds where he had been born, or get strong on the slopes of the hills. . . .

"I've been buying a few things, Jim, and . . . and putting them by. I'll be twenty-three Friday."

"I know."

What was it? What was the other cause of his strange reluctance to say out loud now, "Let's get married before my holidays and have a week at the sea." There was another cause. It would be easy, so simple, to let go and use those words. They would be what he half wanted to say and what Cherry wanted him to say—and yet they wouldn't come. If only he knew the real reason—but he didn't know the real reason. He only knew that there was a force beyond his knowledge or control that held him back in spite of himself. He was waiting for something to happen, and he didn't know what that something was. Once it had happened, he knew that everything would be different and strange but . . . but it, whatever it was, had to happen. It wasn't fair to keep Cherry waiting. It wasn't fair. Walking slowly along the deserted pavements of Saint John's Wood, he came to a sudden decision. He squared his shoulders. Without realising what he was doing, he flung a challenge to fate. He squeezed her rigid arm a little more tightly.

"Listen, Cherry. You know I'm going off to France tomorrow with the chaps from The Hand and Flower."

"Of course I do, Jim. After all, that's why Dad went to get you the 'Broken Column' specially."

"And very kind of him, too. Well now, we'll be back at about half-past ten tomorrow night, and then you and I will have a little talk about the future. Would that be all right?"

"I don't see that there's anything wrong with tonight. Still, if you'd rather. . . ."

He was surprised to hear himself say with determination:

"Yes, I'd rather."

"Very well, Jim. Please don't think that I——" She stopped. "Never mind."

Buoyant because the decision had been made at last and because he had set a time-limit to the machinations of Providence, he said with a hint of bravado in his voice:

"Look. We're passing the very garden where we went last April. Do you remember?"

She softened. "As if I'd forget."

The windows of the bombed house were black and blind in the moonlight and the door hung open to the desolate hall. They stood leaning against the pillars from which the plaster had peeled. Jim kissed her. She could have done with a bit more abandon—if only to have a chance to restrain it. She said at last, blinking into the darkness:

"You like France, don't you, Jim?"

"Oh, I don't know. It was all right there after I was wounded. It wasn't much before. Anyway, I was too scared to notice it until I got hit."

She said scornfully:

"You! Scared! I don't believe you'd ever be scared of anything, dear." She went on, a thread of jealousy in her voice, "What are the French young ladies like? Painted up to the nines, I bet."

"I dunno. Never met any of them. We were too busy."

It was true. The way from Arromanches to the bloody welter of the Fallaise Gap had not been paved with young ladies. Far from it. And the only young lady he had met in France had not been a young lady at all, but a little girl called Marie-Josephe, who had worn a pinafore over her cotton frock, and who had herded the cattle in a Normandy farm and who had sat under a tree and taught him to sing:

"Savez-vous planter les choux,
A la mode, à la mode;
Savez-vous planter les choux,
A la mode de chez nous?"

after they had dug the *Schmeisser* bullets out of his shoulder and the persistent fear of death had subsided. . . . The song came back to him, soundlessly.

"Dad was in the last war and he says that the French young ladies are dressed-up hussies with no decency."

"I don't suppose they're *all* like that, Cherry." He kissed her again. "Not that I care what they're like."

"I should hope not, indeed." She peered at her watch and gave a little gasp.

"It's a quarter to! You know what Dad's like if I'm a minute after the half-hour."

"But you're with me, Cherry."

"I know. But Dad's that strict."

She made her way carefully down the steps, through the weedy garden, out into the lamp-lit, moon-lit road. They walked home in tranquillity. At the door of the greengrocer's, he took her once more into his arms. She said with a slightly businesslike air:

"And we'll have a talk tomorrow—when you come back."

"Yes, Cherry. We will."

"Good. I'll tell Dad."

He took a deep breath.

"Yes. You tell Dad. And now, good night and sleep well." He kissed her with more than his usual warmth. But the moment when she would have welcomed ardour had passed and she drew back. He said a trifle lamely:

"I'm sorry."

"There's plenty of time for that—after tomorrow."

"That's right. Well, good night, Cherry."

She stood quite still in the doorway. He had walked three or four steps before she spoke.

"Jim."

"Yes?"

"Haven't you forgotten something?"

"What have I forgotten?"

"Your parcel." She went on, an edge in her voice. "I would have thought you would have remembered it, specially when

Dad went all the way to his friend to get it wholesale."

"Sorry," he said, "sorry. It's going to France tomorrow that put it out of my mind."

"But that's what it's for! Jim, you are funny."

He kissed her again in the hall. She said breathlessly:

"Don't you dare to have any truck with any French young ladies, Jim."

"Of course I won't. What do you think?"

He was suddenly embarrassed. He wanted to be away from this place and out and alone in the streets. As he walked home, his parcel in his hand, the soundless song became articulate and he stepped to its measure:

"Savez-vous planter les choux,
A la mode de chez nous?"

As Mr. Mitchell heard his daughter's step on the stairs, he switched off the wireless and looked round over his spectacles. She took off her scarf and sat down opposite him. He took out his silver watch and consulted it disapprovingly.

"It's ten to."

She said sharply, "Well, suppose it is. I've been out with Jim, haven't I?"

"Yes you have. That's just the trouble. Has he said anything yet?"

She knew that her father didn't like her smoking, but with great deliberation she lit a cigarette and sat back languorously and crossed her silken knees. His heart sank. This was the grown-up edition of the Cherry he'd once known before, the defiant little girl who wouldn't leave London in the Blitz. If he'd failed to break her then, what chance had he now? In spite of that, a father had his duty and he'd never been one to shrink from trying to do what was right. He said gruffly:

"Put out that cigarette and sit up proper."

"I can smoke if I want to. I'll be twenty-three Friday. And I am sitting properly. Dad!"

"What?"

"Jim did say something. He said he'd talk about the future tomorrow night when he came back from Boolong."

"High time, too."

She narrowed her eyes. She said tersely:

"The point isn't what *he* says any more. It's what *I* say.

Jim's not the only pebble on the beach, and there's as good fish in the sea as ever came out of it."

"What do you mean?"

"I've been steady with Jim Carver for six months now. Oh, I know he's good and kind, even if he does go in for farm talk. The things he says sometimes about bulls and cows would raise your hair. But there are times, Dad, when a young lady wants something more than that, and I'm not sure now that Jim's the man to give it to me. That's what I mean. See?"

He looked at her as if he could hardly believe his ears.

"Have you gone out of your mind, Cherry Mitchell?"

"No, I haven't. You wouldn't understand this, Dad, because you're a man, but I'm going to tell you just the same. It's the sort of thing you won't hear over the road in Saint Saviour's, but it's true. A young lady wants to be wanted—and unless Jim Carver wants me so badly that it hurts him, he's not going to get me." She stood up. "And now I'm going to bed."

"You'll do no such thing. Sit down, Miss."

With an air of bored resignation she sat down. He said with ominous calm:

"Perhaps you'll be good enough to explain what you mean by a young lady wanting to be wanted. What sort of want?"

Her blood was up. She said airily:

"The ordinary sort, Dad. Like you and Mum when you were first married or . . . Frankie Sinatra and Ava Gardner . . . or Solomon and the Queen of Sheba in the Bible. . . ."

He struggled out of his chair, shocked beyond measure, and stared aghast at his daughter. Was this the little girl whose nappies he had changed, the little girl who had sat in her high chair and banged her spoon and spilt her porridge, the little girl who had once said, "I don't like boys. Nasty things!"? And to make it worse, she had dared to bring up people in the Bible. He groped desperately among the Scriptures for a quotation that would devastate this . . . this Jezebel. He found it. He pointed a trembling finger at her.

"The lips of a strange woman drop as an honeycomb and her mouth is sweeter than oil. But her end is bitter as wormwood, sharp as a two-edged sword. Her feet go down to death; her steps take hold on hell." He drew breath. In his hour of need, the apt phrases came thick and fast and he spoke as one inspired. *"Mortify, therefore, your members which are upon the earth."* A tendril of the scent which she always

dabbed behind her ears before she met Jim stole into his nostrils and he blew his nose violently. "*Bring no more vain oblations: incense is an abomination unto me.* Wash yourself and go to bed."

She threw away the end of her cigarette and stood up.

"I'm sorry if I've upset you, Dad. I didn't mean to. But I'm not going to tell you a lie, and that's how it is. If Jim Carver wants me he'd better do something about it—fast. And now, good night, Dad."

His anger evaporated as quickly as it had come. He said in mollified tones:

"That's all right, Cherry. But I won't have that sort of talk in this house."

"O.K., Dad. Sorry I spoke out of turn. Good night."

"Good night."

When she had gone, he sat down again and turned on the wireless. But the programme irritated him and he switched it off. He didn't know what young girls were coming to, with their cigarettes and their airs and graces and their loose talk. Jim Carver was a decent man, with decent wages and in a position to look after a wife. Might even be a kiddie or two one day, and that would be nice. . . . Ah well. She'd be different tomorrow when she'd had a good night's sleep.

"Time, gentlemen, please."

Slowly and with many grumbles, the customers in the public bar of The Hand and Flower allowed themselves to be shepherded into the inhospitable street.

"Good night, Charley. Don't forget tomorrow. Good night, Mr. Hilgrove. Eight o'clock punctual. Good night, Shorty. Good night, Mr. Grenfell. See you in the morning. Good night, good night all. . . ."

CHAPTER THREE

THE crescent moon rose over Saint John's Wood and shone on the slates and chimneys of The Hand and Flower. An amorous cat stropped its back against the locked doors of the public bar and wailed a challenge to the night.

Charley Brewer lay under his blankets, discordantly humming. He couldn't remember the words of the song, but he knew the tune all right and the tune was that of 'Mademoiselle of Armonteers'. He grinned and gave a prodigious wink in the darkness.

"Inky-pinky, parlez-vous."

Luke Grenfell, essayist, dilettante in democracy and honorary proletarian, put down the poems of François Villon and turned out the light. Tomorrow, for a few brief hours, he would breathe the air of the land that had bred that incomparable singer. He whispered in the darkness the opening lines of the 'Ballade of Our Lady', delighting in the exquisite tenderness of the words. "*Dame des cieulx, regente terrienne. . . .*" He thought of the long glory of the French Renaissance, of Charles of Orleans, Ronsard, Malherbe; Joan of Arc rode through his mind in shining armour; he was flung with Voltaire into the Bastille. He heard the song of Roland in the sombre pass of Roncevalles. And all this, all this richness, would be brought nearer to him and more acutely perceived by reason of a Darts Club Outing! The Hand and Flower—*La Main et Fleur*. He smiled and turned over on his side and waited for the ghostly bells of Lorraine to lull him to sleep.

"*A demain . . .*"

When Shorty—who ran for Mr. McIsaac the bookie—left The Hand and Flower, he said good night to everyone except to Mr. Grenfell. He never had had any truck with Mr. Grenfell, and he didn't propose to start, Darts Club Outing or no Darts Club Outing. What the hell Mr. Grenfell wanted to come to Boulogne for at all beat Shorty—when all he had to do was to get into a ruddy aeroplane any moment he wanted to and go off to somewhere posh like Paree or New York.

He walked along Loudoun Road and turned into Belsize Road, to wait for a 31 bus to take him to Kilburn. Two other passengers waited, a Scotch soldier and a girl. A soldier! More like a kid's Christmas tree than a soldier he was, dressed up in a kilt and a tunic with shiny buttons and a pair of white spats like a cissy, and hung all over with brooches and bits of stuff like the stuff you saw in the Bermondsey Market—anything on this tray a tanner. Big bloke, all the same. You'd think from the way the girl was looking up at him that he'd won the Victoria Cross or something. Women were like that: go for anything in uniform, they would. He stopped formulating the ludicrous image of his own sixty-one inches dolled up in a kilt and white spats, and thought instead about Mr. Grenfell, even though every thought hurt him and angered him as if he were biting on a sore tooth.

He'd seen this man whom he hated two or three weeks ago in the West End. Not that Mr. Grenfell had seen him. Not bloody likely. Shorty had been walking up by Berkeley Square on his way to catch the bus from Orchard Street, and he'd passed by a big hotel with flower-boxes in the windows and a flunkey outside. Just at that moment a car had driven up, a three-litre Bentley it had been, and who was driving it but Mr. Grenfell, all dressed up like a dog's dinner, in a soup-and-fish with a dark red carnation in his button-hole. And had Mr. Grenfell been alone? He certainly had not. Mr. Grenfell had had with him the sort of blonde job that kept you awake at nights. She had been wearing a white cloak and golden shoes and flowers in her hair, and Shorty, pressed back against the railings, had heard her say, "I'll go on in, darling, while you put the car away," and Mr. Grenfell had said in his la-di-dah voice, "Right, my angel, I won't be more than a moment," and the flunkey outside had touched his top-hat and said, "Good evening, Mr. Grenfell, sir."

He'd give him 'sir', he would.

Shorty had gone on his way muttering, and the next night Mr. Grenfell had been back in the public bar at The Hand and Flower, dressed in his old tweeds and standing pints of mild to Ginger and Ted and Charley as if he'd never been nearer Berkeley Square than the top of the road. Shorty had told no one of what he had seen. He had stored it up, much as a potential blackmailer might store up somebody's guilty secret. You never knew when it might come in useful. . . .

The bus came thundering down the hill from Swiss Cottage, and Shorty climbed up the stairs to smoke. He sat down on the only vacant seat, beside a girl who was reading a weekly paper devoted to film stars. As the bus started, she glanced at him idly. His face, thin and resentful, was not unhandsome, and she took in the built-up shoulders and the elaborately coloured tie. He intercepted her glance, and saw a flicker of interest in her dark eyes. She turned back to her paper with a gesture as automatic as it was provocative. Shorty fingered his tie. Ah well, no harm in having a go. After all, she'd only seen him sitting down. He looked over her scented shoulder at the open page and ventured a tentative comment.

"Saw Anna Neagle in that last week."

"Oh yes. I think she's lovely."

"She's all right," said Shorty tolerantly. So far so good. "Seen Glynis Johns?"

"Oh yes. I think she's lovely."

"She's a smasher," said Shorty. "Do you like Marleen?"

"Oh yes. I think she's lovely."

"I suppose you go for Trevor Howard, too?"

"Oh yes. I think he's lovely."

It occurred to Shorty's not very flexible or resilient mind that it would be a considerable problem to mention any cinematic demi-god, male or female, who failed to measure up to this girl's only adjective. She was a smashing doll, all the same. A blonde job. A vision of the blonde job he'd seen Mr. Grenfell with manifested itself and walked gracefully down the bus in a white cloak, golden shoes and flowers in its hair. Shorty bit hard on his sore tooth and the vision vanished. He said carelessly:

"I'm off to France tomorrow."

"Yeah?" She didn't believe him. He wished now that he hadn't said it.

"Yeah," he said in his tough voice. "Live far from here?"

"Kilburn way."

"Me, too. Care for a coffee and a fag at the Bridge?"

"I wouldn't mind."

"Okey-doke. Mind how you go."

He let her precede him down the stairs. He watched her,

his eyes glinting, as she swung round the handrail and stepped on to the pavement. Now for it. . . . He jumped off the bus and stood beside her. He saw her face change in the lamplight, change and harden and become contemptuous. Though she was of average height, she was a good three inches taller than Shorty. She looked down at him, and then she glanced quickly towards Kilburn Bridge. She said with an apologetic squirm of her shoulders:

"Oo-oh, there's my girl-friend. Ever so sorry, Big Boy. I must run."

Big Boy!

As Shorty walked alone to the room he shared with Solly Cohen—who worked the Dog Races at the White City—the sore tooth in his mind surged into agony. He knew suddenly why he hated Mr. Grenfell's guts. It was because Mr. Grenfell not only possessed everything in the world that Shorty longed for, but because Mr. Grenfell threw these things away. No wonder Mr. Grenfell wore shabby clothes. He could afford to—because those clothes had cost a lot of dough when they were new. No wonder Mr. Grenfell stooped. He was so tall that he could afford to stoop. . . .

Damn Mr. Grenfell, damn him, damn him. . . .

Anticipation . . . contemplation . . . frustration . . . action.

Trevor Hilgrove was a man of action. He had been accepted as a substitute for Bert Morgan. Fair stood the wind for France—but there was much to do before the dawn.

As he walked home, he sorted out his problems. The first thing to do was to contact his old friend and—er—colleague, Pierre Jumelle. Pierre lived in Paris and was always ready at a moment's notice to supply him with valuable if highly dutiable merchandise. In response to a telephone call Pierre would be delighted to bring his merchandise to Boulogne, and hand it over in return for good negotiable United States currency. Trevor was never without dollars. That part of it was easy.

He let himself into his flat, dialled the Continental Trunk Exchange, asked for a personal call to Monsieur Pierre Jumelle at Paris, Clichy 67-93. There was up to half an hour's delay. Never mind. He would wait. He put down the receiver and lit a cigarette. Gazing absent-mindedly into the middle distance, he weighed up the pros and cons of what he had decided to call 'Operation Timepiece'.

On the credit side was the fact that it would take a pair of very sharp eyes to pick even such a well-known gentleman as Mr. Trevor Hilgrove out of a bunch of darts players on a day's outing. He couldn't possibly have found a better cover for his proposed activities. His next problem was a less easy one. It was that of transporting Pierre's dutiable merchandise from a place A to a place B. He smiled. It was rather from a place B—Boulogne—to a place A—Angleterre! In between places B and A stood that lynx-eyed organisation called His Majesty's Customs and Excise, whose duty it was to scrutinise the merchandise carried by travellers and to levy their toll upon its value. Many persons—of whom he himself had been a distinguished representative—had sought to outwit these guardians of our shores, and a few had been successful—for a while. But the patience of the law was infinite and its arm long, and, sooner or later, these clever people were apt to travel the same road as had Trevor, in the same conveyance, to the same destination—'in the country'. Trevor Hilgrove now gave the most careful thought as to how a repetition of this *via dolorosa* might be avoided.

There were various methods of smuggling, some simple, some complicated. By and large, the simple ones were the best—but practically all of them, good or bad, were known to the courteous officers of the Waterguard. Trevor had considered and rejected some half-dozen subterfuges before the idea of all time came to him.

It was blinding in its simplicity. It was original. It was as fresh as a seagull's egg, laid this very minute. It was suitable, subtle and sure. Moreover, the means of carrying it out were to his very hand. Trevor Hilgrove walked quickly to the cupboard under the stairs, found what he sought, brought it back into the sitting-room and dusted it. A minute examination showed him that this was not just a brilliant idea. It could be made to work. With mounting excitement he went to the tool-box and took out a chisel, a screwdriver and a clawed hammer. He slipped off his jacket and rolled up his sleeves. He was just beginning to work when the telephone bell rang shrilly, urgently, its strident call matching his eager mood. He whipped off the receiver. Would he please hold on for his personal call to Monsieur Jumelle in Paris. *"Ne quittez-pas, Monsieur."* He waited, smiling, his eyes bright.

"*Allo! Pierre? C'est toi, Pierre. Alors, écoute. . . .*"

Trevor wasted no words. Pierre and he had played a similar game before, and there was no need for long explanations. They would meet at three o'clock tomorrow afternoon in the *Café Gerard* at Boulogne. "*Bien entendu.*"

"*Au revoir, cher ami.*"

He put the receiver back and took up the clawed hammer. The amorous cats of Saint John's Wood had long finished their love-making before Trevor was satisfied with his handiwork.

CHAPTER FOUR

Despite her father's optimistic belief that she'd feel different once she'd had a good night's sleep, Cherry Mitchell had no intention whatsoever of letting the sun go down unavenged on her wrath.

Undressing, she had come to a sudden decision. Maybe it was a wicked decision and maybe it wasn't. Right or wrong, she was absolutely determined to go on with it. A young lady had her pride, and she had been put upon for far too long. First there was Jim, Jim with his shilly-shallying, wasting the best years of her life. There was no reason why he shouldn't have said something tonight—if he'd wanted to. What difference could going to France for the day make? And in all these months he'd only kissed her once, *really* kissed her as if he meant it, and on that solitary occasion she'd had to make him, almost. She gazed at herself in the looking-glass, standing in her slip. You'd think a real he-man would be only too ready to slip his arm around a young lady with a thirty-four bust, twenty-four waist and thirty-six hips. Well, if Jim didn't, she used to know plenty as did—and one in particular, one with a motor-bike and a telephone, one who lived in London. It was to this particular one that she proposed to address herself, now, tonight, as soon as Dad was quiet. She'd have to wait till Dad went to bed or he'd be sure to create. Still, Stan Rossiter wasn't the sort that went to bed early of a Saturday night. Far from it. . . .

She removed the day's make-up with cleansing cream, and sat down on her bed to wait until she heard Dad come upstairs. Her resentment about Jim shifted temporarily to her father. What right had he got to tell her not to smoke, and to sit up properly? He hadn't even said 'properly' but 'proper', and if there was one thing she couldn't abide, it was people who talked common. She could smoke and sit how she liked. She'd be twenty-three Friday. A host of real and imagined wrongs rose hotly in her mind, and once again she focused her indignation on Jim. Dad might be old-fashioned and quote great chunks out of the Bible at her, but, fair's fair, what had Dad done? He'd taken a lot of trouble to go specially to his friend in the trade and get the 'Broken Column' wholesale to save Jim a pound. And was Jim grateful? All he'd said was "It's very nice." Very nice, indeed! It was lovely, really lovely and tasteful, too. You'd think a man who was saving up to settle down would be glad to put by a whole pound and say something more than "It's very nice," and then walk off and forget all about it.

She listened intently. She heard Dad stirring, heard the parlour door shut, heard him come upstairs. Say it took him five minutes to get into bed . . . then he'd sit up on the pillows and read 'The Talk of the Day' and the religious article in the *Evening News*. He always read the holy article last thing before going to sleep of a Saturday night. Said it took his mind off business and put him right for Sunday. If she allowed a quarter of an hour in all, she'd be on the safe side.

At a quarter to twelve exactly, Cherry stood up and walked silently on her bare feet across the room, a box of matches in her hand. There was a yellow strip of light from under Dad's door, and she heard the rustle of the newspaper as he turned over the pages. Now he'd reached the holy bit. Very quietly she crept to the stairs and began to go down, holding on to the banisters in the gloom. She reached the ground-floor unheard and went into the shop, feeling her way to the telephone. She dare not put the light on, or Dad might see the reflection and come down. She lifted the receiver and struck a match and dialled. A voice answered immediately. She half-whispered:

"Oh, is that Stan Rossiter speaking?"

"Stan this end."

"This is Cherry, Stan."

"Cherry?"

"Cherry Mitchell. You know."

"Cherry Mitchell!" The voice suddenly became warm and welcoming. "Well, well, well, little Bright-eyes herself—after all these months, and at the witching-hour itself. How's the world using you, Cherry?"

"I'm all right." A respectable girl who'd always kept herself to herself, she was all of a moment overcome with a sense of guilt. Here she was, talking to an old boy-friend on the blower when all she was wearing was her pale blue lingerie sateen nighty and not a single stitch on underneath. Her first feeling of impropriety was immediately replaced by the not at all unpleasant consciousness of sin. She smoothed back her tight curls languidly.

"Listen, Stan. Are you booked up for tomorrow?"

"Well, I *was.*" Stan hesitated. "Anyway, I thought that—that now that you and Jim Carver are sort of dated up, you wouldn't have any more time for little me."

"Jim's going to France tomorrow, Stan, with The Hand and Flower Darts Club Outing. So I wondered, if you were doing nothing. . . . But it doesn't matter to me, I'm sure." She paused and said artlessly, "I can always give old Norman a tinkle."

"You don't want to ring Norman," he said quickly. "You know what they call him our way? 'Norman the Mormon!'"

There was a long pause. She said with what she hoped the French called 'nostalgee':

"After all, we used to have a good time in the old days, Stan."

"Sure, Cherry, sure."

"Still got your motor-bike, Stan?"

"Sure, Cherry, sure."

"Same old bus? Still called 'Lady, be good'?"

"Sure, Cherry, sure."

"Of course, I forgot. Norman's got his two-seater sports-car. . . ."

"Aw, nuts to Norman," he said in American. "Listen, Bright-eyes, how would you like to come on the back of the old bike to Richmond, and then for a row on the briny? I'll ditch the other dame. O.K.?"

"O.K., Stan. I'd like that ever so. I'll meet you at the bus-stop in Baker Street at three. How's that?"

"That's hotsy-totsy!"

"Jim doesn't get back from France till after ten, Stan."

"Then we can go for a bit of a spin on old 'Lady, be good' after we've been on the river. Lady, don't be good. It's nice out on the Guildford Road. Nature and gnat-bites. Oh boy, oh boy, oh boy!"

She suddenly took fright. She said in a distant voice, "Oh, will we, indeed! I don't want any of your gnat-bites. We'll see about the Guildford Road in due course, *after* we've had a blow on the water. Don't you take too much for granted, Stan Rossiter. See you at three."

"O.K. Cheerio, Bright-eyes. Don't do anything you wouldn't like to see photographed—not till tomorrow, anyway. Be seein' you."

"Cheery-bye, Stan."

She put down the receiver, stood for a moment in the dark, fruit-scented shop. Well, she'd done it. Jim shouldn't keep her hanging about, and then go to France and leave her on her own. Dad shouldn't tell her not to smoke. It served them both right, so it did, Jim and Dad. Not that there was any harm in it. Still . . .

Feeling rather like Nell Gwynne, Messalina, La Dubarry and the chorus of the Folies-Bergère rolled into one, Cherry Mitchell began to creep upstairs in her pale blue lingerie sateen nighty.

Only one other member of The Hand and Flower Darts Club was awake at this revealing hour. Jim Carver lay in bed, gazing into the darkness, his hands clasped behind his head. The 'Broken Column' that Cherry had tied up so neatly stood on the chimney-piece, the shape of the parcel curiously like that of a coffin. He had already decided what he would do with it.

He shifted his shoulders. It was queer to be going to France tomorrow. It wouldn't be like last time—thank God! He had been Sergeant Carver then, Sergeant Carver of the 25th Lancers, apt to shoot a bit of a line in other Regiments' Sergeants' Messes, but—let's face it—more scared than he'd ever been in his life. To help him had been the three stripes on his arm and what they meant. He had been well aware that the men in the Landing Craft, amateur soldiers as he was an amateur sergeant, had been watching him, waiting for him to show a lead so that they might follow. They'd followed all right, splashing out of the surf of Arromanches. Sand and wind and the snigger of machine-guns . . . with the thump, thump, thump of the R.A.F. bombing ahead, calling the Lancers on like a muted hunting-horn.

He had been very happy in the Army, looking back. You never realised at the time how happy you'd been, once you'd broken in your first pair of boots and learned who to keep out of the way of. Join the Army and see the world; join the Lancers and scrub it. He hadn't done too much scrubbing, for promotion had come quickly to a good and reliable soldier.

And he'd been around, backwards and forwards over the desert until Alamein, and then it had been forwards for good. More than anything else in the Army, you had your pals. He'd had his pal George Holden, until George had gone over a landmine in a Bren Carrier, and then he hadn't had George Holden any more. Ah, well. . . . That was the luck of the draw, but the Sergeants' Mess had become curiously hollow without George . . . and stayed hollow, what's more.

He glanced towards the chimney-piece where the 'Broken Column' stood. He was glad that it was dark. Queer how things had worked out. All the time he'd been in the Army, he'd planned to go back to the Cotswolds—once Corporal Hitler had been dealt with. It wasn't a big place that his father owned, but a few good acres, over beyond Burford, with a farmhouse mellowed by the weather of four centuries. Windrush-watered and wind-sheltered, the fields were good fields, and the cattle, pedigree Shorthorns, did well on this grass. He'd told George Holden about it many times, showing him, with a rough drawing, the lie of the fields and what he'd like to do. They'd often talked about a sort of future partnership, for George was as land hungry as he was himself. With that strong sense of continuity born into men of their kind, they had known that their work would be of little value unless it were carried on beyond the span of their own lives. Together they had worked out a plan, as amateurish as it was sincere, to get and keep children interested in making things grow. Then, when George had run his Carrier over a landmine, he'd had to start thinking again. There wasn't much satisfaction in doing alone what you'd planned to do with somebody else, and when he'd left the Army he'd been quite content to take a job in London. The Managing Director of the firm was his former Colonel, and to work with him was almost like the old days.

Then he'd met Cherry.

It was at this point that Jim was once again conscious of those nagging doubts that had recently come to beset him whenever he considered his position with this trim and pretty girl. They harked back, these doubts, to something older and stronger than he was. They were rooted in the soil of fields that would, one day, be his. It was the difference between the pavement and the plough. Cherry's feet belonged to the pavements, his to the plough. At first he had tried to approach the subject tactfully, asking her which she liked best, the town or the country. Not realising the real, deep purpose of his question, she had answered him immediately and honestly. She had admitted, with a wholly engaging feminine shiver, that she was terrified of cows, nasty things with horns, and that she was a lot happier to sell the fruits of the earth than to grow them. Sensing his disappointment at her answer, she had swiftly added a corollary—that lambs and calves were ever so sweet when they were little, and that she had had a girl-friend once who had married a gentleman-farmer and that she was quite happy. "Mind you," she added, "my friend lost her looks in no time, and didn't do her nails any more, or anything."

The vision of Cherry herding Shorthorns in a north-easter was a difficult one to imagine, and he gave up trying. You might as well ask him to weigh out a pound of tangerines. And what, in heaven's name, was 'a gentleman farmer'? You farmed land or you didn't—and the best manure in the world was the farmer's boot.

By this time tomorrow he'd have been to France and come back. By this time tomorrow he supposed he'd have fixed things up with Cherry. He even might have done it tonight. What difference could going to France for the day make to his doing what he wanted to do? He told himself that the one thing he wanted, the one thing he would look forward to all day tomorrow, was coming home. Cherry would make a sweet and faithful wife and, given time and tenderness, she might come to love his fields as he did himself. He was a lucky man.

And yet, in the core of his breast, he knew that something was missing. More than that, he knew suddenly that this thing, whatever it was, was very near to him. So near was it, this mysterious, nebulous thing, that he stretched out his hand to grasp it, reaching out into the darkness with eager fingers. In the silence of the night, he heard the sound of his own breathing and the beating of his heart. . . .

The bells of the church sent a flight of melody into the summer sky, and the clock struck one. Before the echoes of the chime had lost themselves in the steeps, Jim Carver had fitted words to the song of the bells:

"Savez-vous planter les choux,
A la mode de chez nous?"

CHAPTER FIVE

"Come all to church, good people,
Good people, come and pray. . . ."

sang the bells of Saint John's Wood as the char-à-banc turned into the Finchley Road.

"Oh, wot a bee-u-tiful morning!
Oh, wot a bee-u-tiful day!"

sang The Hand and Flower Darts Club as the char-à-banc shuddered to a stop by Lord's Cricket Ground traffic lights, honked its horn cheerfully at a devout housemaid hurrying to Mass, surged on to Baker Street and Victoria, gateway to the Continent.

All the club was there as well as Mrs. Collins's four saloon-bar customers. Mr. Hetherington, Mr. Thomson, Mr. Johnson and Mr. Pratt—all gentlemen in the City—sat in splendid isolation in the back seat of the conveyance, a rug spread over the huddle of their knees, while Mr. Hetherington dealt the first of an interminable series of bridge hands. They had frigidly acknowledged the presence of their fellow-travellers and, their social duty done, were getting down with relief to the serious business of the day.

"One no trump," said Mr. Thomson.

Unlike the four City gentlemen, Trevor Hilgrove was very much one of the party. With a nice sense of the fitness of things, he had brought a dart-board with him and four sets of darts. "After all," he had said with a grin, "it might rain over on the other side and then you chaps might like a game. Show the Froggies a thing or two." Nobody else had thought of bringing so apt and so genial a symbol, and it was generally agreed that Mr. Hilgrove was a very thoughtful gentleman and that it was a pleasure to have him with them. He carried the dart-board slung over his shoulder, plain for all to see, and in his hip-pocket had been a flask of whisky which was now passed from mouth to mouth with the utmost cordiality. Though the back seat refused with some acerbity, Mr. Hilgrove was generally considered to be all right.

"I've got a bee-u-tiful feeling
Everything's going my way. . . ."

Charley Brewer tapped the spittle out of his mouth organ and raised his bowler-hat with great gallantry to a passing Rolls-Royce. He was dressed in a blue serge suit, an open-necked shirt and white gym shoes. A peach-coloured rose sprouted from a metal vase tucked into his buttonhole, and a heavy brass watch-chain described a semicircle from one waistcoat pocket to the other. He replaced his bowler, took a deep swig from Mr. Hilgrove's flask and handed it to Jim Carver. Jim smiled.

"No, thanks, Charley. Bit too early in the morning for me."

"All right, mate. Pass it on to Mr. Grenfell there—and then back to me."

Jim Carver handed the flask to Luke Grenfell who, albeit with a feeling of nausea, took a sip. He was determined at all costs to enter into the spirit of the outing. He buried his face tactfully in his handkerchief, spat out the whisky and passed back the flask with a grin that was slightly sickly.

"How delicious, Charley."

"My best respects to your lordship, I'm sure."

Baker Street . . . Portman Square . . . Oxford Street . , , Marble Arch. . . .

Jim Carver held the parcel that Cherry had wrapped up for him so carefully, and frowned. He held it gingerly, as if it were a thing that he disliked touching with his hands. This instinctive repugnance gave him a slight feeling of disloyalty to Cherry. It wasn't her fault, not in any way. She'd done her best, but the thing was she'd never known George. If she had known George, she too would have understood that this was the last thing on God's earth that he would have liked. Never mind. Once they were aboard ship and well away from the harbour, he'd dump it over the side and get what he really wanted in Boulogne.

It had been a queer night—and an even queerer morning; for the thought that had come to him with the chiming of the bells had still been with him when he woke. It was that he was nearer than ever to an overwhelming delight, a delight that was somehow linked to the rhythm of a song. He had sung it to himself as he had shaved, he had been made buoyant by it, it had threaded itself into the radiance of the morning. He turned to Luke Grenfell, his grey eyes smiling.

"Do you know a French song called *'Savez-vous planter les choux'*?"

"Of course. It's as old as France. Why?"

"I just wondered. I can't get it out of my mind."

"I shouldn't try."

"No, I don't think I will."

Trevor Hilgrove held out his gold cigarette-case and, after a momentary hesitation, Jim took a cigarette. Trevor lit it for him with a practised flick of his lighter. Odd thing, Jim didn't care for him very much, in spite of his geniality and his generosity. Perhaps it was because he fitted into every situation so immediately and so smoothly. Let's be fair. He'd nothing against Hilgrove. Absolutely nothing.

Park Lane . . . Hyde Park Corner . . . Grosvenor Gardens. . . .

"Now, Gentlemen, you've all got your passports and your money? I've got the tickets and when we get to Victoria I want you all to keep together. Charley, you can't both play your mouth-organ and smoke a cigar, so you'd better make your mind up which you're going to do. Shorty, you all right?"

"I'm all right."

"Cheer up, Shorty. We're all out to enjoy ourselves."

"I said I was all right, didn't I?"

"You O.K., Mr. Grenfell?"

"Rather!"

"Right. Off we go. Charley, would you give me a hand with this crate of Guinness? Fine. Now, let's all stick together. Pardon me, Inspector, are we right for the excursion train to Boolong? O.K. Thank you, Inspector."

A whistle blew, and the train slid almost imperceptibly along the platform to the accompaniment of cheers from The Hand and Flower Darts Club. The Thames was broad-breasted in the morning sunshine, and a tug with its attendant string of barges chugged upstream to Putney, Strand-on-the-Green, Richmond. Soon the houses fell back from the railway-line, and the trim gardens turned into fields of green, fields of ripe corn, heavy branched orchards with their trees sagging under the weight of apples. Sevenoaks—with white streamers of blown steam flowing past the carriage windows —Ashford, hop-fields, oast-houses, horses on holiday galloping ponderously away from the rushing train. . . .

"Oh, wot a bee-u-tiful morning,
Oh, wot a bee-u-tiful day. . . ."

"Double four hearts," said Mr. Pratt.
"Re-double," said Mr. Hetherington.

It was queer how the song persisted, the other song. Jim fitted its cadence to the sound of the wheels of the train, and he sang it silently to the beat of their drumming. It occurred to him that it had nothing whatsoever to do with what he ought to be thinking about. With a sudden mental effort, he wrenched his thoughts to one side, holding them strongly and steadily away from the siren song, so that the wheels of the train seemed to alter their beat. Deliberately he tried to project a picture on to the screen of his mind. It formed slowly and with difficulty, but once he had forced it into focus, he had to admit that it was one that might well quicken the pulse of any man.

It was a picture of Cherry Mitchell: Cherry on her father's arm, Cherry blinking her kitten eyes demurely behind a white veil, Cherry moving slowly on satin shoes up the aisle of the church where he waited at the altar. *"I James, do take thee, Cherry . . ."* and then the triumphant rolling of music in the roof . . . tum-tum-terruptum tum-tum . . . a hired Daimler with white ribbons fluttering . . . *"Pray silence for Mr. William Mitchell, father of the bride . . ."* a shy and shimmering Cherry holding his arm . . . *"May all your troubles be little ones. . . ."* Cherry going upstairs, Cherry coming back, no longer dressed in shimmering white but in the sort of clothes he knew, Cherry getting into the Daimler, confetti in Cherry's hair and an old shoe trailing from the back of the car. . . . Cherry and he alone . . . Cherry looking at him sideways from under her lashes . . . a girl secretive . . . his wife revealing . . . a girl different.

The pictures' edges blurred and Jim Carver looked down the corridor of the years. He'd be very happy with Cherry, and it would be a continuous comfort to know that she'd be waiting for him to come home every night from the office, looking as she always looked, clean and fresh and neat. Let the Cotswolds winds blow over the wet fields, let others herd the Shorthorns, let other hands draw milk from their bountiful udders. A man couldn't have everything, and he was well content. . . .

And, then, without warning, the song came back, tapping gently on the shut door of his mind and set his blood dancing once more. Smiling, he opened the door and the song dwelt within him. . . .

"Folkestone Central. Remain in your seats, please. Next stop Folkestone Marine. Have your passports ready, please."

There was a light wind blowing over the harbour and the sea was up, up and dancing and sparkling and lovely to look at. Gulls swerved and floated in the bright air, calling plaintively, and alongside a great ship's masts rocked with every surge of the tide.

"Charley, don't get wandering off. You can get a packet of fags on board. Come on, Shorty; come on, Mr. Grenfell. You lead the way, Mr. Hilgrove."

The Immigration Officers were very quiet and courteous.

"Good morning, Sir. British? May I see your passport, please? How much money in notes are you taking out with you? It is an offence to take out more than five pounds."

Trevor Hilgrove put down his dartboard and made as if to turn out his pockets. He said with a rueful grin:

"Five pounds! I've almost forgotten what five pounds looks like!"

The Immigration Officer smiled sympathetically.

"That's how it is with a lot of us, Sir." He glanced at the dartboard. "Going to take on the French in a darts match?"

"That's the idea. Show them how!"

"Good luck to you. Next please. Good morning, Sir." It was Charley. "British? May I see your passport, please. . . ."

"Oh, my God," said the Purser to the Chief Steward, "here they come."

"Pretty to watch, Cyril, pretty to watch."

One after another, The Hand and Flower Darts Club climbed the sloping, corrugated gangway and stepped on to the deck. Trevor Hilgrove looked around him with the slightly patronising air of a man who knows the ropes, and made his way aft, Charley Brewer took off his bowler to the Purser and enquired. "Where's the bar, Mate?" and the Purser said humorously, "I'm not the mate, Mate, I'm the binnacle. Second companion aft, starboard side and mind the step." Fred Collins, looking more like a Buff Orpington than ever, clucked and fluffed after his errant chickens. "Mind how you go, gentlemen. That's the stuff, Mr. Grenfell. Shorty, nobody's going to bite you. *Not* that way, Charley. The gentleman said 'aft' and that means the back of the ship. Anyone seen Mr. Hilgrove? Jim, you got everything? Listen, Charley, can't you bloody well read? It says 'Passengers are *not* allowed on the bridge'. Oh, pardon me, Captain, I'm sure. . . ."

With the conscious air of being sheep among goats, Mr. Hetherington, Mr. Thomson, Mr. Johnson and Mr. Pratt made their way to the first-class saloon and sat down.

"Unless my memory fails me," said Mr. Johnson, "you had just led a spade, Mr. Pratt."

The gangways were lowered, the last ropes splashed into the sea and a host of gulls swooped to hover and pick and cry over the gushing bilge. The ensign, which had fluttered at the vessel's stern, stiffened and blew in a quivering rectangle of colour, spread by the wind, as the ship's bows cleared the harbour and drove steadily over the sunlit sea to France.

Jim Carver drained his glass of light ale and turned away from the bar in the ship's saloon. They must be about halfway across, and now was the time to do it. He had left Cherry's parcel on the floor in the corner and he took it up and carried it very carefully up the steep stairs and on to the deck. The wind was cool and fresh in his hair as he made his way aft and leaned on the rail. There were few people about, so he thought he'd wait a bit until no one was looking. The wide spaces of the sea seemed to stretch from the rim of the sky to the rim of the sky, and the wave-tips were flecked with white. He glanced forward, and watched with delight the bow-wave surging outwards, being held by the pulse of the tide, swinging back to dissolve under the ship's keel in a bubbling lather of foam. Cherry's parcel was balanced precariously on the rail. No one was looking. With a sudden thrust of his hand, he pushed the parcel away from him. It turned over and over as it fell, splashed into the seething wake, sank, bobbed up again, and was carried astern, dancing derisively on the surface of the sea. Well, that was that. . . .

"Hallo, Jim. Dropped something?"

Jim Carver swung round on his heel. Luke Grenfell, his hair blown backwards and his eyes watering in the wind, was standing beside him. Jim said slowly:

"Yes. I'm afraid I have."

"Bad luck. Anything valuable?"

Jim gazed at him. He didn't know this chap very well, and yet, in spite of that, he suddenly and instinctively knew that Luke Grenfell was the one person who would understand. Now that he'd done it, he wanted very much to talk about it to someone, and, by doing so, to banish the persistent feeling that he'd let Cherry down. He took a deep breath.

"Well, it was valuable, in a way. And in another way it wasn't. I'll tell you if you like. But I warn you, it's a long story."

"I'd like to hear it, if you'd like to tell me."

"Yes, I'd like to. Let's get out of the wind."

They sat side by side, looking out over the swinging sea.

"Cigarette?"

"No, thanks, Jim. I only smoke *Gauloises*."

"I know them. They're the French cigarettes in the paper packets. About that parcel. I didn't drop it overboard. I threw it."

"That seems very odd. You were holding on to it so carefully in the train."

"Yes, I know." He braced himself to tell the story, and he told it, with long, inarticulate pauses. "Well, it's like this. When I was in the Army I had a friend called George Holden. We volunteered on the same day, in '39, and, oddly enough, we stuck together right up to '44. We came out of Dunkirk together, got our three stripes together and were sent out to the Middle East. Then, after the desert, we were together in Syracuse and landed in Italy from the same Landing Craft and went up Highway Six in the same Armoured Brigade." He paused and said apologetically, "Sorry to talk all this service stuff. Must be pretty boring to a civilian."

"But I wasn't a civilian, Jim. I was in the Navy."

Jim glanced at him in sharp surprise. Somehow he had never imagined this man in uniform, any uniform. But the knowledge that he had served—in any capacity—made the telling of the story a lot more easy. He said, smiling:

"I suppose you were an officer—Sir."

"Yes, I was actually, at the end. But I had three years first as a rating. Go on about your friend George Holden."

"You—a rating!" he said with curiosity. "Where did they send you?"

"All over the place. Mostly to Russia—to deliver the sinews of war to Uncle Joe. Murmansk and back. But about George Holden. . . ."

"You did Russian convoys. That can't have been funny."

"It wasn't. You'd just reached Highway Six, in the same Armoured Brigade."

"Were you ever sunk . . . Mr. Grenfell?"

"I answer to 'Luke'. Yes, I was sunk. Twice actually. The first time I was picked up almost at once, the second time they took rather longer. Not funny at all. But I'd like to get back to Sergeant Holden."

"Does Shorty know that you were in the Navy?"

"Shorty? Shouldn't think so. Why should he? No point. But we're out of Arctic waters now and cracking up Highway Six. What happened then?"

Jim Carver was silent for a minute, screwing up his eyes in the bright sunshine.

"After Italy we were pulled home again to refit and we trained in the south. They asked George and me if we'd apply for commissions, but we both said that we were quite happy where we were, in the Sergeants' Mess, after all that time. We went to France on D-Day. Everything was all right until the Falaize Gap. I got hit, but George bought it."

Luke Grenfell said in a low voice:

"What filthy luck, Jim."

"It wasn't good. He ran over a land-mine in a Bren-gun Carrier, and it hurt him quite a lot. But you couldn't kill George easily, and he lived for a time. He finally died in a hospital in Boulogne. He's there now."

Far over the sea, on the port side, Cap Gris Nez was indefinite in the summer haze. The wind had dropped a little and it was more easy to talk.

"Go on, Jim."

Jim Carver looked away and lit another cigarette, taking a long time over it. He said finally:

"You know Cherry Mitchell? Well, I told her all about George Holden, and that I thought I'd take this chance to go to Boulogne and up to where he is, and make sure that he's all neat and tidy and leave a few flowers. He never could resist flowers, George couldn't," said Jim Carver truculently, "so much that he did seven days Jankers in '41 for knocking off a bunch of roses from the Officers' Mess garden." He laughed shortly. "That's George Holden, that was. Well, Cherry told her father, who's in that sort of business and, with the best will in the world, Mr. Mitchell went to see a friend of his in the trade and got a thing on the cheap."

"What sort of thing did he get?"

"As far as I know, it's called a 'Broken Column'. It's made of flowers and the end is sort of snapped off to indicate death. There was a little stuffed bird perched on the top, and that was supposed to be George's soul on its way to heaven. If George wasn't dead and saw that, he'd die laughing. But as he is dead, it wasn't the sort of thing that I thought he'd like."

"It sounds pretty grim."

"It was."

"So you tipped it overboard."

"Yes. Anyway, George never liked things that had been got on the cheap."

Luke Grenfell frowned. He blinked rapidly behind his horn-rimmed spectacles.

"And I don't think that you do either, Jim." He paused and said abruptly, "I'm going below for a drink."

"I'll stay up here for a bit."

Jim walked, glad to be empty-handed now, to the rail and gazed over the sea. France was quite near. From Cap Gris Nez a long low line of hills, sand and foam-fringed, swept back in a great curve towards the mounting cluster of Boulogne, the *Haute Ville* dominated by the high dome of the Cathedral. Yellow sand-dunes on the port side—and to starboard the etched promontory of Cap Alprech, falling steeply into the sea. He took a long breath of the shining air. He was suddenly alert and excited, and the words of the song came back and back into his mind, and he sang it to himself, smiling:

"Savez-vous planter les choux,
A la mode de chez nous?"

"Jim, the Governor wants you down in the saloon. All the boys are there."

"Coming."

Jim Carver walked aft with a springing stride and went below. Mr. Collins greeted him portentously:

"Ah, there you are, Jim. Now we're all here—except my saloon bar customers, who are looking after themselves. Now, Gentlemen, have you all got your landing tickets?"

"Yes, Mr. Collins."

"All got your passports?"

"Yes, Mr. Collins."

"And you've all got your money?"

"Yes, Mr. Collins."

"So far so good. Now, Gentlemen. I've got one or two things to say, and I'd be grateful if you'd pay attention, please. Charley, for God's sake put that blasted mouth-organ away. You've time and to spare for that. When we land, you give up your landing tickets, show your passports, and go into the Customs and come out at the other end. Is that plain?"

"Yes, Mr. Collins."

"Then we all walk up together into the town to a place called the Eatoile Hôtel, where we have middle-day dinner. There's tomato soup and roast beef and cabbage and chips and treacle-tart arranged, and there's Bass and there's Guinness and they've promised us a good feed. Then, after dinner, we'll maybe have a bit of a sing-song and maybe a walk around and a look at the shops until the boat goes back at a quarter-past six. The great thing is for us to stick together and not go wandering off." Charley Brewer contemplated the ceiling and scratched his ear. Mr. Collins went on darkly. "France isn't England and England isn't France, but we'll all be all right so long as we stick together. You listening, Charley?"

"I'm listening, Mr. Collins."

"Right, Gentlemen. One last word. Suppose one of us does get wandering off on his own—and I sincerely hope he won't —he's got to be at this ship at ten-past six punctual. O.K.?"

"O.K."

"Now, Gentlemen, keep yourselves to yourselves, and if any French try to get talking to you, say 'No Compree' and sugar off. We're on our own and we don't want any truck with foreigners. Got me?"

"We got you, Mr. Collins."

The Hand and Flower Darts Club flooded up the companion-way to gaze over the ship's rail. Outside the entrance to the harbour there was a cemetery of ships. The sunny waves lapped over the black and broken hulls and swirled through rusted plates. Over the town, the painted lifebelts of the *Calvaire des Marins* shone white, a blackcloth of circles to the bronze Christ at whom the fishermen always glanced in supplication as their craft put to sea. Napoleon's column was as slender as a pencil—and the houses were not like English houses. They were tall and narrow and their windows, the shutters thrown back, flashed like diamonds.

The ship described a slow, majestic half-circle in the sunny harbour, passed the tortured concrete of wrecked submarine and E-boat pens, slowed up to come alongside the quay. Ropes were flung, whipping through the air like angry snakes, were caught, made fast. The porters in their blue blouses and berets jabbered and gesticulated and grimaced as they hoisted the heavy gangway and stood back to await their prey.

"Now, Gentlemen, don't forget. Stick together—and keep ourselves to ourselves."

Charley Brewer was first down the gangway, and his white gym shoes did a little dance on the cobbles of Boulogne. He was followed by the knowing Mr. Hilgrove, by Mr. Collins and by Jim Carver. As he stepped ashore, Jim touched Mr. Collins on the arm. He said quietly:

"I've got a little job to do before lunch, Mr. Collins, a private job, so don't worry about me. I'll come and join you at the Etoile when the job's done." He smiled and said reassuringly, "It's all right. I won't get lost. I've been here before."

"Ah, you've been here before, have you, Jim?"

"Yes, Mr. Collins. I've been here before. . . ."

CHAPTER SIX

"Saint George he was for England, Saint Dennis was for France;
Sing honi soit qui mal y pense." THOMAS D'URFEY, 1681.

JIM CARVER came out of the Customs Hall and stood for a moment breathing in the smell of the harbour. A little man with a peaked cap and a number of gold teeth sidled up to him with an ingratiating smile, and asked in comprehensible English if he could be of assistance.

"Yes, I think you can." Jim was suddenly shy. He shifted his feet and said lamely, "I'm going to have a stroll and a drink, and then, sometime, I'd like to find the cemetery where the British soldiers are. You know. Sometime. After I've had a walk round and a drink."

"You desire which place, Monsieur?"

"The sort of cemetery place." It occurred to him that George Holden would split his sides laughing if he could see him now. He said doggedly, "What I want is the cemetery where they put the British soldiers who were killed. *Compris?*"

"You desire the *Cimetière*?"

"Yes. That's right. I've said so three times. The *Cimetière anglais.* Where they buried our chaps."

The man looked at him with sudden understanding.

"I understand your words, Monsieur. Me also, I was a soldier." He drew himself up with a touch of pride. "*Artilleur, moi.* But"—he shrugged—"the *Cimetière* is not a very gay place, not even on a day of sunshine. You will be more 'appy in a café, in *Chez Poupette* for example, which is gay all the time. But it is as you wish. . . ." He turned and pointed. "You go by this way and then you cross over the bridge. You see *la Cathédrale*? It is more 'igh than that. You climb upwards all the time. Wait. You desire a taxi? It is better you go in a taxi. I 'ave a friend 'oo 'as a taxi."

"No, thanks. I'd rather walk."

"As you wish. You walk on foot. When you arrive in the town, you ask someone."

"What do I ask for?"

"Wait. I write it for you. Then you show the card to some-one and 'e . . . she will speak you the direction. I give you now my card." He wrote the words 'CIMETIÈRE DE L'EST' in spidery capitals on a grubby card that had on the front

MAURICE SEVRIER
Taxis: All informations:
English spokken: Specialities

"*Voilà, Monsieur.*"

"Thanks very much." Jim hesitated. "Cigarette?"

"Thank you very much, Monsieur."

"Take the packet. And thanks again."

"It was a pleasure."

He turned as Charley Brewer, first through the Customs, emerged from the *Buvette,* having celebrated his arrival in France with two large glasses of Benedictine, topped up with Green Chartreuse. With a practised and expectant eye, Maurice instantly took in every detail from bowler-hat to drooping rose, to gym shoes. *Ah ça! Ca—c'est bien lui! Ce—c'est vrai!* He swept off his peaked cap and every gold tooth took on an extra sparkle.

"*Bonjour, Milord!*"

"Speak English, Mate?"

"Oh yes. Very good. I 'ave many friends, all English people. All English people 'oo come to Boulogne know me, English lords, ladies, sirs, all sorts. You desire steak-and-ship, seelk stocking, some post-card? You desire French *parfum,* bananas, French liqueurs?" He drew breath. "I fix for you, everything at a true price. We do not buy from dam-robbers. O.K.?"

"Listen, Mate," said Charley Brewer, "listen to me. . . ."

He whispered confidentially in Maurice's receptive ear. Maurice heaved a deep sigh, and his face took on a look of the deepest dolour. He spread his hands in despair.

"*Il . . . n'y . . . a . . . pas,*" he said with finality. "They . . . do . . . not . . . exist. Not since the war. In this respect Boulogne is dead. But one day, this dam-fool *gouvernement* is finish and we 'ave again in Boulogne—I 'ope. But, pay attention, Monsieur. When we 'ave bought seelk stockings, *parfum,* banana and post-cards, we go together to *Chez*

Poupette and we look. I 'ave many friends, and, 'oo knows, we find per'aps someone. O.K.?"

"Charley Brewer," said the voice of Mr. Collins wearily, "did I tell you, or did I not, to keep yourself to yourself?"

"I was only asking this gentleman a civil question," said Charley bitterly. "Only a civil question."

"Well, pack it up and come on with the boys. You don't want to miss your nice dinner, do you?"

"Sugar my nice dinner," said Charley. He lifted his bowler to the disappointed Maurice. "Stick around, Mate, and maybe I'll see you later."

Jim Carver walked slowly along the quay-side. The air was heavy with the smell of fish and of the sea. He looked across the water, through the tangle of masts and spars and brown nets drying, to where the hotels and cafés had once stood with their striped awnings and their bay-trees in pots and their little round tables, the checkered tablecloths fluttering in the wind, and their teeming life. Where were the sunburned, black-shawled, white-aproned women who used to sit behind their laden stalls of silver fish straight from the sea, with live, blue-black lobsters crawling over the gasping, gill-dilating piles, and buckets of strange, submarine creatures? Where were the spread coloured umbrellas of the flower-market and where was the shouting? "*Voici des belles fleurs, voici des huîtres, voici des bas-de-soie pour Madame. . . . Tout frais, tout frais, tout frais. . . .*" Here was desolation. Weeds grew from the rubble of the Hôtel Splendide, and a hungry bitch, heavy in whelp, nosed and scratched in what had been the proud kitchen of 'Le Folkestone'. As far as the eye could see stretched the broken levels of war, grey as they were forlorn.

Jim stopped by the bridge. A strident poster had caught his eye, and he translated it with much frowning. The text was dominated by a drawing of a German soldier, such a German soldier as Jim had never seen in five years of war. The face, encompassed by a steel helmet, was lean, scowling and brutal, and the angular hands gripped a *Schmeisser* automatic. "Do you want this again?" asked the poster. "Demand total disarmament in Germany and the appointment of a Russian Commander-in-Chief. Join the Communist Party of France."

He looked around him, at the stricken port and at the

desolate *quais*. It was usually in surroundings such as these that the Kremlin chose to sing its siren song, for the mother of Communism was not *la mère* but *la misère*. He looked at the poster again and smiled. It was very properly stuck to the rusty shield of what was charmingly called a *chalet de nécessité*!

And now for the town, some flowers and George Holden. As he crossed the bridge, he began to practise what he would say to the shopkeeper. "*Bonjour, Madame. Je veux les fleurs pour mon ami. Combien, s'il vous plait?*" He could do the asking all right. The trouble was that the French talked so damn fast that he couldn't understand a word of the reply, and he never knew how much they were asking him for. He'd pay with a thousand franc note—for flowers couldn't cost more than that—and simply take the change and say "*Merci beaucoup*." And he'd given the chap at the harbour all his cigarettes so he'd have to get some. French cigarettes were called *Gauloises*, and they were in blue packets and Mr. Grenfell smoked them. That should be easy. With great temerity he stopped at a tobacco and magazine kiosk presided over by an elderly lady in black satin and began to marshal his French. To Jim's mingled discomfiture and relief, the woman at once addressed him in fluent Cockney and sold him a packet of *Gauloises* wrapped up in *Les Nues des Folies-Bergère*. She also directed him to a florist which was open on Sundays and on the direct way to the *Cimetière de l'Est*.

It was queer to see the motor-cars driving on the right and to hear the piercing note of their horns. They scurried about the streets like frightened rodents, and it seemed to Jim that accidents were avoided by a continuous series of miracles. He wouldn't care to be a bobby on point-duty in Boulogne. No fear. Another queer thing was to see great sides of beef in the shops and veal and pork, free for all to buy—provided people had the money. Compared with the brooding emptiness of the harbour, here was great animation. Women and girls, their prayers said, looked in the shop windows and greeted each other, shaking hands. There was a terrible lot of hand-shaking and hat-raising, even among the men. Carefully following the directions given him by the woman in the kiosk, Jim made his way past the stone prison with its narrow cobbled bridge over a long-dry moat and its forbidding door, turned up a sloping hill and saw a café on the corner. It stood back from the road, in the shadow of chestnut trees, and its name was the *Café des Marronniers*. The woman had said that he would find a florist opposite this café, and, sure enough, there it was. He paused for a moment to run over his meagre French, and then boldly entered the shop. Inside it was cool and moist after the hot sun outside, and the air was scented by many flowers. An old woman, sitting in the back of the shop, gave him a brief, perfunctory smile.

"*Monsieur?*"

The words that had come so readily to his tongue outside, now fled; he said, stammering:

"*Je veux des fleurs.*"

"*Bien,*" she said without interest, "*nous avons des roses, des œillets, des hortensias, des pensées. . . . Quelle sorte désirez vous, Monsieur?*"

In this horticultural catalogue, Jim clutched desperately at the one word he understood.

"*Les roses . . . s'il vous plaît.*"

The old woman smiled again and stood up, and waddled over to a vase of red roses. As she picked them out, one by one, she asked, looking round:

"*Combien de roses voulez-vous, Monsieur? Elles coûtent quatre vingt dix francs la pièce. Vous en voulez une douzaine?*"

How much did that make? Oh hell. It didn't matter. He said, not knowing at all what it would cost:

"*Oui, oui. A dozen.*"

"*Bien, Monsieur.*"

The roses were dark red and lovely on their long, thorny stalks. The old woman shook them, and a shower of tiny drops of water flashed across the shaft of sunshine and sprinkled the tiled floor. She held up the flowers for him to see.

"*Voilà, Monsieur. C'est pour offrir?*"

Now what the hell did that mean? Were they to offer? Of course they were to offer. Did the old vixen—the Cotswold word came readily—did the old vixen think he was going to wear them in his button-hole, or throw them away? He said, with a thread of irritation in his voice:

"*Oui, oui.*"

"*Bien. On va faire un joli bouquet.*"

She waddled back to the counter and took a large sheet of

cellophane and some green string, and began to make up the roses into the sort of ghastly thing that men give to film stars. Jim watched her, frowning, not realising at first what she was doing. He said sharply:

"Ce n'est pas nécessaire."

"Mais c'est pour une dame."

Oh my God! The old woman thought he was buying flowers for his girl-friend. He struggled to find the words.

"Non, non. Ce n'est pas pour une girl-friend. Non. Pas une dame. Non. Pour mon ami."

She looked at him strangely. *"Pour votre ami?"*

"Oui, oui. Pour mon ami dans le . . . le . . ."—he glanced wildly at the card Maurice had given him—*"dans le Cimetière de l'Est. Mon ami est un anglais soldat qui est mort.* Sergeant George Holden, 10132012, 28 Troop, C Squadron, 25th Lancers. Now *fini. Mort. Compris?"*

The old woman gazed at him for a full minute without speaking. Under that steady gaze Jim's muscles stiffened and relaxed. Suddenly, to his astonishment, she smiled in a manner that was wholly kind, wholly understanding. In a flash he had become a person in her eyes. Carefully she folded up the crumpled paper and put it away, and wrapped up the roses in plain white paper. She held them out to him:

"Voilà, Monsieur."

"Merci beaucoup. . . . Um . . . combien?"

"Rien du tout, Monsieur."

He didn't understand. He said:

"Oui, oui. Mais combien?"

She said in a soft flow of words:

"J'ai dit—'rien du tout'. C'est avec plaisir qu'on offre les fleurs de France pour le tombeau d'un soldat anglais."

He stared at her. From the shadowed back of the shop a man's voice spoke gutturally. Jim had not seen that there was anyone there.

"My wife says that it is a pleasure to offer, to give, the flowers of France for the grave of an English soldier."

"Your wife is very kind." Jim lifted his hand, let it fall helplessly. "Very kind."

The man came out of the shadow. He was perhaps fifty, plump and in his shirt-sleeves. He held out his hand, announcing his name.

"Baptiste Cottet."

"My name's Carver. Jim Carver."

He shook hands with the man and with his wife. He was sorry he'd thought of her as an old vixen, damn sorry. He said, "Look, I don't mind paying. Honestly."

"No. We are very proud to give. You are English?"

"Yes. English."

"You will find many English up there." He jerked a thumb towards the hill. "I was with the English. *Ils se sont battus comme des lions.* They 'ave fought like lions. If you wish to give, to pay something, give to the Cathédrale, *pour les pauvres.* There are many poor people in Boulogne, Monsieur Carver."

"I will, and thank you again." He was very much embarrassed. He held out his hand. "Well, good-bye. Or as you say here, *au revoir.*"

"*Au revoir, Monsieur.*"

He was out in the sunny street, the flowers in his hand. And there were people about who said that the French were mean. . . .

"Now, Gentlemen," said Fred Collins, "we're all here with the exception of Jim Carver, who's got a bit of private business to attend to, and dinner will be in in a minute. Charley, it's no good asking the waitress anything. She can't speak English. Do come back and sit down. We'll carry on with the tomato soup without Jim. Now I'd suggest a nice glass of sherry all round, and then there's Bass and there's Guinness. You don't want to start in on the old *vin rouge.* Charley, for God's sake, come and sit down. I tell you, she can't speak English. . . ."

"She don't 'ave to," said Charley.

The wind that had dropped earlier in the morning was rising again as Jim walked through the open gates of the *Cimetière de l'Est.* Somewhere among these acres of polyglot dead lay George Holden, and it occurred to Jim that George would take a bit of finding.

The French graves really were a bit much. Stone cherubs, looking slightly decadent, clasped their carved fingers and stared sightlessly upwards, poised for flight. There were squadrons of petrified angels, dozens of agonised Christs, a host of open Bibles, some of them with actual photographs of the deceased let into the stone. Gave you quite a shock, in a way, to see a picture of the chap himself. Brought it home to you. Jim stopped by one of these and read the inscription: On the right-hand page of the stone Bible was engraved: "*Victime du Gestapo le* 28 *avril* 1943." And on the left-hand page, "*Michel Dessalle, Séminariste,* 1920–1943." A priest, too. His photograph, glazed to protect it from the ravages of wind and weather, gazed upwards from its setting in granite. It was a solemn face, wearing incongruous horn-rimmed spectacle. It wasn't unlike Luke Grenfell. "*Victime du Gestapo.*" Poor devil. Jim walked on. He saw a long avenue of shaven grass, very fresh and green, and made his way to it. It ran between rows of graves, the ones on the right being French, and on the left British. The British were very neat and formal. Each sunken tombstone had a name and a military cap-badge carved into the stone. Here lay Riflemen, Camerons, Connaught Rangers, Royal Engineers, Australians, Grenadiers, Canadians, Hussars, New Zealanders, Gunners; there was hardly a regiment or a corps that gave allegiance to Britain that had not sent a representative to sleep on this hillside over Boulogne—thirty years ago. Jim had looked at many of the graves before he realised that these were the men who had died in the war to end wars, and that he must search elsewhere for George Holden, who had bought it in the last scramble, in the war to begin wars. He stayed for a little while. There were wallflowers and great tight clusters of blue and purple and orange-coloured flowers whose name he didn't know. The wind off the sea was fresh and cool and there were larks singing. A chap could be in a worse place.

With great diffidence, he asked an old man wheeling a barrow if he could direct him to the *anglais soldats qui est morts dans la guerre avec Hitler.* Like so many people in Boulogne, the man spoke English. He set down his wheelbarrow and said:

"Please come. I will show."

As they walked along together, the man talked. He spoke of conditions in Boulogne and how bad they were. "We were bombarded by everybody, English Navy, R.A.F., Germans, Americans. It was not good to be in Boulogne then and also today it is not good." They passed by a square of grass bare as a tennis court, and Jim asked what it was. It looked so very empty in this tangled forest of tortured stone. The man said shortly:

"The Germans were there. Now they have been *exhumés* and taken home—out of France. It is better so."

"Yes. I suppose so."

Women, most of them dressed in black, moved quietly along the pathways between the graves, carrying jugs of water and scissors and flowers. They were as remote as nuns. The man stopped by a stony pathway and pointed.

"There you are, Monsieur. Your compatriots—and mine. *Au revoir.*"

"*Au revoir.* Thank you very much."

Jim walked along the pathway, past the lines of crosses, reading each name. Here was one inscribed simply, "Unknown British soldier," and beside him, as if by chance, "*Soldat français inconnu.*" Well, those two would certainly have a lark, swopping identity discs . . . upstairs. There were a lot of R.A.F., a hell of a lot, and a lot of R.A.F. (Polish) as well. The Sappers and the R.A.S.C. hadn't done too well either. Suddenly Jim stopped dead. Hells bells, there was old George at last.

His grave lay beside that of yet another "*Soldat français inconnu.*" There was a huge mound of purple round the base of the cross, and Jim noticed with detachment that the wind was blowing all the time, stirring the box hedge behind and that a lark was still singing. He said softly, affectionately:

"Hallo, you old bastard."

His regimental number slanted on the upright of the cross, with his name on the horizontal and the date of his death below. 10132012 Sergeant George Holden, 25th Lancers, 10.12.44. Yes, that was right. All correct, Sergeant. He'd nothing to put the roses in, no vase or anything, so he thought he'd just leave them on the grave. As he bent down, he was aware that he was being watched—and by a woman at that. Unlike most of the women about the cemetery, this one was quite young and not in black. Pity she'd nothing better to do than to watch him. He wished she'd push off and mind her own damn business. Oddly enough, the dark red roses went quite well with the purple cluster. He straightened his back and stood in the sandy path, looking at the grave, his head on one side. It looked all right. He'd taken rather longer than he had thought searching for George, and the Darts Club would be wondering what had happened to him. He'd better begin to think about shoving off. No good hanging about. He said under his breath, "Well, bung-ho, George," and turned abruptly.

The woman was still there. He passed within a yard of her, marching rather than walking now. As he stepped out she spoke to him.

"Excuse me, please."

He didn't want to talk to anybody then, man or woman; he stopped and swung round on his heel. He said curtly:

"Yes. What do you want?"

She came towards him. She wore a summer frock and she was young, about twenty or twenty-one. Her eyes were long-lashed, and she was dark and she walked with great grace. All that he saw in a moment of time. She stood opposite him, looking at him with a candid glance.

"Excuse me, please. But you are Sergeant Carver, Sergeant Jim Carver of the 25th Lancers?"

He stared at her.

"Yes. I . . . I am. Well, as a matter of fact, I'm not Sergeant Carver any more. I'm simply Jim Carver. But . . . who are you?"

Suddenly her eyes danced. She held out her hand, laughing.

"I am Marie-Josephe."

CHAPTER SEVEN

Jim Carver looked with unbelief at the graceful girl who stood facing him, her sunburned hand outstretched. High in the upper air, the singing of the larks was thin and of great sweetness, rising and falling with the eddies of the wind. Almost with reluctance, he took her hand in his. It was cool and firm. He said to her, his lean face solemn:

"But you can't be Marie-Josephe. Marie-Josephe is only a little girl."

"She was a little girl. Now she is a lady. She is . . . is grown up."

He was still holding her hand. He said suddenly "Sorry," and let it go. He gazed into her face. He saw the smooth forehead and the sleek brows; the irises and the pupils of her eyes and their lashes; he saw the sensitive nostrils and the tiny, delicate, down-curving lines in her lips. He saw the almost imperceptible pulse that beat in her throat and the division between her breasts, and the thin gold chain with a medal of Our Lady that lay there. He said slowly, shaking his head, smiling:

"I still don't believe it."

"You wish me to prove to you that I am who I say, that I am Marie-Josephe? Wait. I will do so." She looked around and waved her hand as if to encompass the vast host of the dead. "They won't mind. Listen, please."

He knew instantly what he would hear and he heard it. Her voice was small and husky.

"Savez-vous planter les choux,
A la mode, à la mode?
Savez-vous planter les choux,
A la mode de chez nous?"

"Now do you know?"

"Yes, now I know. I know, but I still find it hard to believe that it is really you. You are so . . . so——"

"Explain."

He lifted his hand. He said lamely, conscious of her springing body. "You are very different. Of course, come to think of it, it is seven years. But I have always thought of you as you were, in a cotton frock and a pinafore. You wore that medal then, too, the same one. I remember so well your cotton frock and your pinafore."

"And you were in khaki uniform with a black beret with a badge of two . . . two lances and the King's crown. When you went away, you gave me the badge to wear. I have it still."

"That's true. I gave you mine and I took George Holden's cap-badge instead . . . when he didn't need it any more."

"You have not changed at all. When I saw you, I was nearly sure immediately. Then when you stood up and did not walk but marched, then I was quite sure. It was like when you made a parade in our orchard, before you ran to your tanks."

"But you must have known thousands of soldiers, of our chaps."

"That is true. But only one gave me the thing from his beret, the badge of two lances with the crown of the English King. So I always remembered Sergeant Jim Carver—of the 25th Lancers. Please, what are you doing in Boulogne?"

"That's a long story and I'm only here for the day. We all go back tonight, on the 6.15 boat. It's a thing called a Darts Club Outing, and it's to do with a pub in London, a pub called The Hand and Flower."

She shook her head, mystified.

"What is a Darts Club?"

"It's a sort of game we play in pubs, in The Hand and Flower."

"*La Main et Fleur,*" she said softly. "That is very pretty. The game I don't understand. And why do you play this foolish game in the *Cimetière de l'Est*?"

To his astonishment, he heard himself say:

"You have become quite like a flower yourself, Marie-Josephe. And I don't play darts here. I came to see a friend, the man whose cap-badge I wore . . . . Well, not to see him personally, but to see where he is. I've just left the place." He wrinkled up his eyes in the bright and windy sun. "What are *you* doing here?"

"Come. I will show."

He walked beside her along the sandy path, glancing at her, frowning. She walked as if she were listening to hidden music. Once she caught his glance, holding it for a moment and then looking away. She stopped at the end of a row, the same row in which George Holden lay. She said:

"There. That is why I have come."

It was a cross, as simple as old George's; it said: *"GUERRE* 1939–1945. *DENIS BERTHIER. Soldat Français. Mort pour la France."*

Jim Carver said carefully:

"Who's he?"

"My brother, Denis. He was killed in the Resistance in 1943. He was working with the *Cheminots,* the Railwaymen of Lille. He did many things against the Germans. He was only nineteen years."

"Then your name is Berthier?"

She said smiling:

"*Oui, Monsieur*. Permit me to introduce myself. *Mademoiselle Marie-Josephe Berthier*."

"I only knew you as Marie-Josephe. Now that you are . . . are grown up, I suppose I should call you Mademoiselle."

"That would be very foolish of you, Sergeant Jim."

"I'm not Sergeant anybody. That's all over. I'm Jim."

"And I am Marie-Josephe. For always to you, I am Marie-Josephe. Where is your friend?"

"He's quite near your brother, oddly enough." He walked a few steps and halted. "There's George Holden."

She stood looking at the grave with its dark red roses. She said:

"Those beautiful roses are from you?"

"Yes. No. Well, I mean, they were meant to be. But when I went into the shop to buy them, the woman thought they were for some girl-friend or other, so I had to explain that they were for old George here. Then she wouldn't take any money. She absolutely refused. So they are really from her."

"No. They are from you." She stated a fact, a truth, without emphasis.

"I suppose so, in a way. But that's what happened. Her husband, the old woman's husband, I mean, said I should give something to the Cathedral instead. He said that there were a lot of poor people in Boulogne. I thought I'd do that after lunch."

"That is very wise. After lunch we will go together."

He said in some embarrassment:

"But listen, Marie-Josephe. I've got to lunch with The Hand and Flower Darts Club at the Etoile—and there are no ladies in the party. I mean, the boys are waiting for me now."

She looked at him steadily, candidly. She said with simplicity:

"You will please come with me, to the farm of my father. It is impossible that you do not."

They were still standing staring at George Holden's grave. Jim Carver stretched the fingers of his right hand. It was a strong hand, and he rejoiced in its strength. The larks were still singing like mad and the wind was blowing.

He said, "Of course."

She had come in an antiquated Renault, the tyres of which were worn as smooth as silk. The paint was dusty and blistered, the bonnet was fixed to the chassis by a length of twisted wire, and a spring stood out from the burst upholstery. Marie-Josephe said with a soft chuckle:

"It is not very elegant, not at all like an English Rolls-Royce. On the contrary. And the thing to make the engine start is broken. So if I sit inside, please can you turn the . . . the handle in front. Then the engine will go."

"May I look at your starter?"

"Of course. But it is broken. *Cassé*."

He unwound the length of wire and lifted the bonnet and bent down to examine the engine. She watched him with a curious expression. In a moment he straightened his back.

"Have you a spanner and a bit of insulating tape?"

"I don't know what those things are. But in the back under the seat there are many things. Come, we look together. All I know of motor-cars is that they require *essence* and oil and water."

She opened the door with its broken and rusted hinge. Jim dragged the seat out and put it on the grass verge. He took off his jacket and rolled up his sleeves. He said to her gaily, confidently, absorbed in the physical task before him:

"After all, I used to mend tanks—and this will only take five minutes. You can sit inside if you like and read the paper."

"No. I will watch you. I prefer to watch you."

"Right. Off we go."

As he worked, he talked to her. He was very happy to be using his hands and his muscles in the knowledge that Marie-Josephe was watching him. "You see this cable here? It runs from the battery to the starter motor, and it's been rubbing against the edges of the flywheel. So I'm going to cut out the frayed bit and rejoin with insulating tape. It's a piece of cake." Funny how the old slang of the squadron came back readily to his lips. "An absolute piece of cake, Marie-Josephe, that's what it is. I suppose you haven't got any pliers. No? O.K. It doesn't matter. I can do it with my penknife. Tell me, how long has the starter not been working?"

"Oh, for a long time. For many months. By the farm we have a little hill, and in the winter we push the car and it runs down the hill and the motor starts. Jim."

"Yes."

"You have not said a word, a single word, of how I can speak English. Tell me, please, if you think my English is not good."

"I think it's marvellous." He twisted the wires of the severed cable neatly together and began to unroll the sticky tape. "We'll be through in a minute. Where did you learn your English?" He grinned. "All I taught you was 'Hurry through the gap, chaps, and press on regardless'. Do you remember?"

"Of course I remember," she murmured softly. " 'Hurry through the gap, chaps, and press on regardless'. I never knew what it meant. I still don't really know."

"It's a sort of joke we had at Alamein. Not really funny at all. But tell me about your English."

"It is quite simple. I was at a day school in Boulogne with nuns. There I learned the words, but my accent was terrible. When I left I was sixteen, and I still took lessons, in English and in dressmaking and in how to play the piano. Then, every summer, we had an English lady to stay at the farm for one, two months, and I talked with her all the time, to make my accent less terrible."

"But why did you want to learn English?"

"I don't know. But I did. I wanted to learn English very much."

He pressed the insulating tape firmly round the cable and stood back.

"That should be all right," he said with a wholly engaging

touch of pride. "Now, if you'll just hop inside and press the self-starter, we'll see what happens."

She got into the car and sat down and looked at him with bright eyes.

"Ready?"

"Yes. Ready."

She pressed the self-starter with her thumb. A surge of power flowed along the mended cable and the engine started with a splutter. She shook her head, laughing.

"I think you are a wonderful man, Jim. For a long, long time a thing is dead, and then you come and, all in a moment, it is alive again. I find that very strange."

"Do you? Keep the engine running, and I'll put back the seat. Do you live far away?"

"No. Not far away."

"You know, I've got to catch the boat at a quarter-past six."

"Yes. I know." As she glanced at the watch on her wrist he saw the flash of a diamond on the third finger of her left hand, and the brightness went out of the sun.

The road was flat and slate-blue, undulating like a cobra between forests of pine. There were goats in the deep grass, and buttercups in the fields where the forests fell back. Jim pointed to the needle quivering in the dial on the dashboard and said in laboured tones:

"You see? Your battery is charging again."

"I see. Is that a good thing?"

"Yes. That's a good thing." He gazed ahead through the cracked windscreen at the loping road and the flying telegraph posts. After a little while, he pointed at her hand.

"Tell me about that. Your ring, I mean."

"My ring. Oh yes." She glanced at her left hand gripping the steering-wheel, and saw with surprise, as if she had never seen it before, the diamond on her finger. She said after a pause, "That. Oh that. It was given to me by my fiancé."

"So you're engaged, Marie-Josephe."

"Yes. I am engaged."

"I hope you will be very happy."

"I hope so also."

"Who is he?"

"His name is Henri Dubot. He is a *notaire,* a lawyer, who lives in Boulogne. You will meet him. He will be today for lunch at the farm of my father." She looked steadily ahead, not speaking. Then she said in a small voice, "And you, Jim?"

"Me?" he said quickly. "Me?"

"Yes. You. Surely, after the years, you too——"

"Of course." He saw Cherry Mitchell through the cracked windscreen, Cherry on her father's arm, Cherry in shimmering white, Cherry blinking, Cherry putting out her hand to be held, Cherry desirable, Cherry accessible, Cherry submissive, Cherry rooted in the land he knew, Cherry English, Cherry safe. . . .

"Of course. Me too." He went on, in a strong defensive voice. "I'm going to marry a London girl called Cherry Mitchell. So there we are, Marie-Josephe. Both of us engaged."

"Yes, we are both of us engaged. It is very happy for us." She went on talking, making words. "It is a beautiful day today. Our fields begin here. The spring was not good and we had much rain—so much rain that the ground was full of water, and it was difficult to . . . to——" She sought for the word and he gave it to her. "To plough." She went on. "That is the word. That is right, 'to plough'. It was difficult to plough. Now it is much better."

He looked over the sunlit fields and a Cotswold farmer spoke.

"Yes. But even so, some of your barley is flattened. You must have had a lot of rain and a south-west wind."

"Yes. That is true." She accepted his knowledge of wind and weather without comment or surprise. She was thinking of a person and not of the elements. "Tell me of your Mademoiselle Mitchell. Is she young and very pretty?"

Jim said obstinately:

"Yes. She is young and pretty. She is fair—and very pretty. What's your Monsieur . . . Monsieur Dubot like?"

"You will see him," she said shortly. She slowed down the car and turned and looked at Jim steadily. "The farm of my father is near, less than one kilometre. When we have had lunch, we will go together to Boulogne, you and I. You promise?"

"Of course. After all, I don't even know my way back."

"I will show you. We will go together. Say 'I promise'."

"I promise, Marie-Josephe."

"Good. Now here, on the left, is the farm of my father. When we go together to Boulogne, you will tell me more of your Mademoiselle Mitchell."

CHAPTER EIGHT

Saint John's Wood woke up grumpily, stretched itself, remembered that it was Sunday morning and turned over to give itself another blessed hour between the sheets.

But sleep refused to come back to Cherry Mitchell. She had woken early after a very bad night, a night ridden by unquiet dreams, and now she lay in bed, sharply awake and sharply aware of a nagging sense of guilt. Over and over again she found herself making excuses, trying to minimise what she had done. After all, what did it amount to? All she'd done was to 'phone up a boy she'd known for years and ask him to take her out for the afternoon. No harm in that. No harm at all—nor would there be, either. And if Jim Carver hadn't gone off to France with The Hand and Flower Darts Club, it simply wouldn't have entered her mind even to give Stan a tinkle, much less make a date with him. It wasn't as if she liked him—not now, anyway. He'd been all right in the old days, she supposed, with his motor-bike and the way he had of singing the words of the music in her ear while they were dancing. He certainly could waltz, could Stan. She didn't suppose there was a better waltzer than Stan in the West End of London. And when he did that special scissor step of his, well, you were just wafted away in his arms. Once she'd made Jim Carver take her to a dance. . . . Once and once only, thank you very much. But in spite of all he'd got—and he'd got plenty—Stan Rossiter wasn't a patch on Jim. Not a patch. Actually it would be quite easy to ring up Stan again and say that she was sorry but that she'd forgotten she had another date all the time. But Jim shouldn't go off to France and leave her—even if it was really to see where his friend was. And he'd been ready and willing to spend two pounds ten on flowers, and he hadn't been a bit grateful for the fact that she'd saved him a pound. You'd think pound notes grew on trees, the way Jim was ready to chuck them about the place for someone who'd died years ago, anyway.

Half-past nine. Jim must be well on his way by now, and Dad would be waking up soon and wanting his cup of tea and the papers. Funny how fond Dad was of the Sunday picture paper, with him being so holy. When she'd asked him about it, he'd been very angry at first, and then he'd said that there was no merit in being good unless you knew how bad other people were, and that the things you saw in the Sunday picture paper made you pray all the harder. He'd refused to discuss it any more, and she had had to be content with this undoubted piece of sophistry.

Just on twenty to ten and it was a beautiful day. It really was. Just the right sort of day for a spin on the back of a motor-bike.

Cherry got up and took the multifarious pins out of her hair and brushed it till it shone. She washed and did her teeth, and put on her dressing-gown and her slippers. Then she tiptoed downstairs, took the papers from the letter-box, and went into the kitchen and put the whistling kettle on. While waiting for it to boil, she looked at the pictures in the middle page. The one on the left caught her eye immediately, and she gazed at it critically. It was the photograph of a young woman in a Bikini bathing-dress. She stood on the end of a diving-board, her arms raised as if she were about to plunge into the sea. As there was no sea visible for her to plunge into, Cherry assumed rightly that she had taken up that posture for another purpose—to show off her figure. The headline to the picture was "Oh la la!" and the caption read: *"The girl who put the 'amour' into 'glamour'—Mademoiselle Fifi Delacourt of Boulogne."*

Boulogne!

Only last night she had told Jim that the French young ladies were a lot of dressed-up hussies. Well, 'dressed-up' was hardly the right word, not for this one, anyway, the shameless thing. And Boulogne was the very place Jim had gone to, as he said, "to see where his friend was." No wonder he'd taken thirty-bob's-worth of flowers with him. She examined the picture of Miss Delacourt from head to poised toe with ever-increasing venom, and it was then that the kettle chose to set up its shrill whistle. To Cherry's overwrought imagination the sound exactly resembled the wolf-call made by amorous soldiers on the prowl, and she whipped off the kettle's spout and banged the teapot on the tray. Her half-formed decision to cancel her appointment with Stan Rossiter vanished utterly, and she was determined to teach Jim a lesson. She made the tea, tucked the paper under her arm and marched upstairs.

"You awake?"

"Yes. I've been awake this long time. Lovely morning, Cherry."

"The morning's all right. There's your tea and the paper."

"Good girl. Sit down, dear."

She removed his trousers from the back of the armchair, and sat down in silence while her father opened the paper. She knew instantly what he was looking at and her mouth tightened. After he had looked with great care at the photograph and read the caption, he pronounced judgment.

"*'All wickedness is but little to the wickedness of a woman.'*"

"That's all right. We're not all like that."

"It says in the paper that this . . . this woman comes from Boolon." He looked at his daughter over his spectacles. "That's where Jim's gone."

"Well," she said sharply, "what of it?"

"I only remark on the fact. Bit of a coincidence, that's all. No need to take on."

"I'm not taking on. Some people got no decency, that's all."

"Meaning who?"

"Meaning the young lady—so called—in the photo that you've been looking at for the last five minutes. That's who."

Mr. Mitchell rapidly turned over the page. For want of a suitable retort, he said with a touch of peevishness:

"Did you put any sugar in my tea?"

"I did. Plenty."

"Doesn't taste like it. Ah well. What's for breakfast?"

"I could do you an egg."

"An egg'll be nice. I suppose Jim and the boys'll be getting near Boolon by now. Funny going all that way, to Boolon, just for the day."

"I don't see anything funny about it."

"You got out of the wrong side of your bed this morning, Miss!" He went on in warning tones, "You better mind your manners by the time you get to your Aunty Flo this afternoon."

Aunty Flo! Cherry's jaw dropped. She had clean forgotten about Aunty Flo, that terrible old woman who lived at Muswell Hill and whose tongue was as swift and as forked as an adder's. On the mercifully infrequent occasions when Aunty Flo summoned the Mitchell family, father and daughter, to

Muswell Hill, the Mitchell family toed the line and went. The childless widow of a prominent North London tradesman, she was reputed to have money put by—and no dependants. Although Cherry clearly had expectations, she always approached Muswell Hill with a feeling akin to terror, for tea with Aunty Flo was less of a social affair than a surgical operation. Before Cherry had had time to take her hat off, the preliminary probings had begun. By the time Cherry reached her second cup of tea and her first piece of cake, she had been stripped and laid on the operating-table, and the scalpel was nicking away at the delicate shrouding membrane, revealing the infected spot with uncanny, instinctive accuracy, waiting to slide in and cut it out and lay it on a plate among the tomato and cucumber sandwiches for leisurely dissection. To visit Aunty Flo with a clear conscience was an ordeal. To enter her house with Stan Rossiter on her mind would be suicidal.

With a great effort, she kept her voice casual.

"Oh, Aunty Flo. I'd forgotten about her. Well, I can't go, not this afternoon I can't."

Mr. Mitchell went on reading the paper as if he had not heard. Then it seemed as if her words had suddenly penetrated. He looked at her incredulously:

"What did you say?"

"I said I couldn't go to Aunty Flo's, not this afternoon. I've got a date."

"You've got a date!" He shook his head. "You got a date."

"That's right, Dad. I got a date." Though her knees were trembling and her heart fluttering, she looked steadily at her father. "So that's that."

Mr. Mitchell sat up in bed. He flung the Sunday paper on the floor. It so happened that the photograph of Fifi Delacourt fell upwards and caught Cherry's eye. In an odd way it stiffened her resolution. Her father said thickly:

"You will come with me to your Aunty Flo's this afternoon. That's all. Now go below and cook my breakfast."

"I'll cook you your breakfast, Dad. But I can't go to Aunty Flo."

"We'll see about that, Miss . . . and give me back the paper off the floor."

Cherry stood up and gathered the pages together. She gave the paper to her father. He took it with a grunt. She left the room with what dignity she could muster. Nothing on earth was going to stop her meeting Stan Rossiter now. . . .

She refilled the kettle and put it on the gas-ring, broke an egg into a cup. Dad liked his egg fried both sides. While she waited for the grease to melt in the pan, she buttered three slices of bread and began to lay the tray. She didn't want any breakfast herself. The very sight of food made her feel queer. She went about her task mechanically, her mind far away from what she was doing. She was planning, down to the last stitch, what she would wear when she met Stan. Up to this morning she'd meant to put on her old wine corduroy shorts and her leather jacket and her beret—all things that Stan knew and approved of—because she was going on his motor-bike. But now she was out for blood. She'd teach Jim Carver—and Dad—*and* that French hussy, come to that. She'd wear her nylons that she'd bought from the boy with the crinkly hair and the attaché-case outside Selfridges. They'd go well with her peep-toe wedge sandals. She'd put on her new flowered art-silk frock that she'd got at C. & A., and she'd carry her swagger coat in case it was chilly out on the Guildford Road. A touch of rouge and a lot of lipstick, her pink lace gloves and a dab of *Nuits de Passion* behind each ear, her red and green 'Jungle' scarf—and Stan Rossiter would certainly get an eyeful! The fact that this ensemble was flagrantly unsuitable for pillion riding deterred her not at all. If anything it was an incentive.

Dad's breakfast was ready. She carried the tray upstairs and entered his room. Mr. Mitchell's not very swift brain had had time to ponder the implications of his daughter's pronouncement. He said with ominous calm:

"Sit down, Cherry."

She put the tray on the bed and sat down.

"You say you got a date this afternoon."

"That's right. I have. That's what I said."

"And Jim Carver's gone to Boolon with the boys."

"I know."

"You told me last night that when Jim came back tonight, you and he were going to get engaged. Is that right?"

"Not quite, Dad. I told you that we were going to talk about it."

"Same thing."

"No it isn't. Not by a long chalk, it isn't."

Mr. Mitchell was unwilling to reopen the subject of his daughter's views on being wanted. With a considerable effort he kept his temper.

"Who's your date with?"

"A boy."

Mr. Mitchell choked. When he could trust himself to speak he said:

"Who is he?"

Cherry wrapped her dressing-gown a little more tightly round her. Now for it. . . .

"That is a matter which I prefer not to discuss."

"You . . . you refuse to tell me!"

"Sorry, Dad, but I do."

Ten, twelve years ago, the day the air-raids began, he had packed his little daughter off to the safety of the country. The next afternoon she had come back, having travelled over a hundred miles by herself to return to the inferno of London. She had told her father then that she had been thinking about it, and that she wasn't going to be turned out of her home to please Hitler or any other nasty foreigner, come to that. Again she had been cast forth, again she had returned, trembling but determined. This time he had beaten her, beaten her in the cellar while the bombs crashed on Saint John's Wood and the fire-engines jangled through the burning streets. Then they had said a prayer together—and Cherry had stayed. He saw that same little girl today, and the knowledge of his own impotence to bend the steel spring within her sent a surge of anger to his finger-tips. Suddenly he became articulate. He shouted at her:

"Go to your room this instant minute, Cherry Mitchell, or I . . . I——"

"I have no wish to remain here."

She stood up. This time her dignity was not assumed. It was very real. As she walked out of the room, her father jumped from his bed. Cherry crossed the landing. He seized her by her shoulders and flung her violently into her room. He wrenched the key from the inside of the lock and slammed the door with a bang that shook the window-pane. Cherry half-stumbled to her bed and sat down, shaking. She heard the key rattle in the lock, the lock click and the key withdrawn. Through the thin panels of the door, her father shouted at her furiously:

"Pride goeth before destruction and a haughty spirit before a fall. There you are, Miss, and there you stay till I take you to your Aunty Flo's."

Once again the church bells called the good people of Saint John's Wood to come and pray, but Cherry Mitchell, imprisoned and sitting on the unmade bed of what had become her cell, was unable to answer their summons. She heard Dad's step on the stairs and then the hall door shut, and she knew that he had got dressed and gone to Matins.

When the bells ceased their calling, Cherry got up and tried the door. She did so automatically and without hope. It was securely locked. She pursed her lips and crossed the room and looked out of the open window.

Between the sill and the little yard, with its door into the lane, there was a sheer drop of about twenty feet. Cherry looked to her left and to her right. On the right there was a rusty black drain-pipe that made a right angle about three feet below the window, and then ran perpendicularly down to the yard's brick wall—and to freedom. Cherry measured the drop, shuddered and went back to her bed.

The house was very silent, and even the sounds in the sunny street were muffled. Cherry gazed at the locked door with narrowed eyes. She became conscious of an unfamiliar emotion, of a mounting, impersonal resentment against the deprivation of liberty. There was no longer any thought of Stan Rossiter in her mind. His puny image had faded against the grievous, academic wrong of imprisonment without trial. The blood that ran in her veins was English blood, and the distillation of the centuries had thinned it not at all. What was the thing she had learned at school and thought to have forgotten long ago, a thing called Magna Carta and 'have his carcase' or something?

It all boiled down to the fact that Dad had no right to lock her in.

And long before Runnymede, where Magna Carta was signed, there had been that British queen, what was her name? Oh yes, Boadicea, queen of the Iceni, bleeding from the Roman rods, who sought with an indignant mien, counsel of her country's gods. . . . And after her, Elizabeth of England who'd been put in the Tower of London once, but had got out and become Black Bess . . . or was that someone else? And Florence Nightingale with her lamp, and Mrs. Pankhurst. A throng of half-remembered, hitherto unrealised ancestors, English all of them, rose up and beckoned Cherry Mitchell to the window, and she went on faltering steps.

She looked down to the sunny yard and imagined, with terrifying clarity, a crumpled figure lying there waiting for the ambulance to come from the hospital and lift her up on a stretcher to take her away.

What say the reeds of Runnymede? The wind moved them and they rustled dryly, whispering in her ears. Cherry drew a deep breath, filling her lungs with the English air. With great deliberation she went away from the window and opened her chest of drawers.

Boadicea, queen of the Iceni, in an Etam bra and girdle; Elizabeth of England in an old-rose slip-and-pantie set; Florence Nightingale in nylons; Mrs. Pankhurst in pink lace gloves; Cherry Mitchell in a new flowered art-silk frock. But the scarlet finger-nails that Cherry touched up with her polishing pad were the nails of Grace Darling, broken and bleeding at the oars. She put on rather more rouge than usual, because her cheeks were as pale as her courage was high. She found a pencil and an old receipt from C & A Modes and wrote a brief note to Dad. She wrapped her green and red Jungle scarf and her wedge sandals in her swagger-coat and dropped them out of the window into the yard. They seemed to fall a terribly long way, and the thud with which they hit the ground made Cherry feel even sicker than she felt already. Briefly she commended her soul to God. She went back and added a postscript to her note. Then she climbed out of the window and felt for the angle of the drain-pipe with toes enclosed in the nylons she'd bought from the boy with the crinkly hair and the attaché-case outside Selfridges.

Corporal Marvin P. Lewes, United States Air Force, late of Maine (New England) and now of Pinner, Middlesex (England), swung his Jeep round the corner of the road and slammed his brakes on hard. He had seen an electrifying sight. From a first-floor window of a house, a young woman came out backwards, feeling with her toes for the angle of the drain-pipe. Despite the modernity of his speech and appearance, Corporal Lewes burned with an old-world chivalry. In less than thirty seconds he was standing at the bottom of the drainpipe, his muscular arms outspread. He looked up, half-expecting to see the furious and frustrated face of Stalin himself at the window. Instead he saw a remarkably shapely pair of nylon stockings and quite a lot of an old-rose slip-and-pantie set. With true New England chivalry, he averted his eyes and called upwards, "O.K., you can drop right now."

Cherry looked down desperately—and did so.

CHAPTER NINE

The farm stood to the left of the road on the brow of a smooth hill. There were black-and-white cows in the wide pastures, and a field of wheat was turning from green to gold in the valley below. At the summit of the hill, Jim looked back and saw, far away, the shining levels of the sea, broken only by the great helmet of the cathedral of Boulogne.

Marie-Josephe turned through an open gate into the farmyard and put the brakes on. As the car shuddered to a stop a huge, shaggy dog launched itself from one of the outhouses and bounded forward, jumping on the running-board. Marie-Josephe put her hand on his head.

"This is Siki. In the night, he is the best and most savage watch-dog in the *Pas-de-Calais.* Please make friends with him."

Jim got out of the car and advanced cautiously. Siki flattened his stomach against the ground and bared his teeth, growling and twitching his tail. Marie-Josephe joined Jim and began to talk softly, reassuringly, speaking in French. "You are a foolish fellow, Siki, a very foolish fellow, for this is our friend, Jim." She patted the dog's head. "This Englishman will not do any of us any harm. He is very welcome to *Clos d'Argent.*"

The dog's eyes flickered from Jim to Marie-Josephe. The growling died away in his throat, and the stiff body relaxed.

"Now go to him. He will not do you any harm."

"Are you sure?"

"Quite sure. At least, I am very nearly sure."

"So be it, Marie-Josephe. Even though I feel rather like Daniel——"

"Who is this Daniel? Is he also an Englishman?"

"No. A prophet in the Bible. He's the chap who hobnobbed with lions."

She laughed. "Oh yes, I know. Be like Daniel and—'press on regardless.' "

"Here we go."

Jim advanced steadily. He stretched out his fingers and laid his hand firmly on the shaggy head and scratched behind

Siki's ears. After a moment, Siki began to sniff at Jim's ankles. Then, as if suddenly making up his mind, he lifted his head and licked the back of Jim's hand with his pink tongue. Marie-Josephe laughed with delight.

"You see! The prophet Daniel has made a great victory over the lion. You and I are both his friends. He will be like that with you now for ever while it is daylight. From Siki you have the . . . the freedom of *Clos d'Argent*. It would be different at night."

"Is that the name of the farm?"

"Yes. *Clos d'Argent*. It means 'the field of silver'."

"It is a very pretty name for a farm, Marie-Josephe."

"I am very happy that you like it. Now come and I will present you to my mother and to my father and to my grandmother and . . . and to my fiancé. But first, I will put Siki on his chain."

"Quite unnecessary. Look." He passed his hand gently, unhesitatingly over the dog's mouth and Siki jumped up and put his paws on Jim's chest. He smiled proudly. "You see."

"Yes, I see. But, all the same, I must put him on his chain." She faced Jim. Her eyes were bright and brimful of laughter. All of an instant the years between them had gone and she was once again the little girl in the cotton frock, singing in an orchard about how to plant cabbages. It was a brief and startling glimpse, and then maturity closed around her again. She said solemnly:

"Siki, alas, is *contre la loi*."

"What do you mean?"

"He is against the law. He is a rebel. He does not like *notaires*, lawyers, very much."

"That must be . . . be very embarrassing for you," said Jim huskily.

After the bright sunshine, the hall of the farmhouse was dim and cool, as dim and cool as the inside of a wine-bottle. Jim followed Marie-Josephe along a tiled passage. As he did so, he was conscious of a strange sense of repetition. The simple act of walking behind Marie-Josephe along this tiled passage was deeply familiar to him. He had done it before. Maybe it had been a thousand years ago, but he had done it before. He was absolutely certain of that. He knew with ancient clarity the set of her shoulders, the movement of her shoulder-blades and of her hands, the articulation of each separate vertebra in her spine and the infinite grace of her carriage. He knew that she would turn to the right after two or three more steps, and that there would be a picture on the wall, a sombre, steel-grey print, and that there would be an oak door through which they would go.

All these things were exactly as he knew they would be.

There were four people in the room, two women and two men. They were sitting at a large round table, and Jim saw that there was one vacant chair and that a place had been laid for lunch. He hesitated awkwardly at the door for a moment, and then Marie-Josephe took his arm and led him forward. As the two men stood up, she said gaily:

"You will please forgive me that I am late, but I have for you a very big surprise. I bring with me an old friend. Maman, you will remember Sergeant Carver, Sergeant Jim, of the Lancers."

Jim found himself shaking hands with a calm-faced middle-aged woman in black. She said with great courtesy:

"Monsieur, one must admit that . . . among so many English. But you are extremely welcome."

"Thank you, Madame."

"As you see, my mother speaks English very well, much better than me. Also my father. Papa, you will remember Sergeant Jim Carver, who was with us. His tanks were among the apple trees and he used to help to make the butter."

"Of course." Monsieur Berthier was a tall, spare man with an immense bushy moustache. "We had many English with us, Mr. Carver, but I am sure that I remember you. You were very kind to Marie-Josephe. You are going to stay to lunch with us, naturally."

Everything would be all right—as long as they went on talking English.

"Thank you very much. It's very kind of you."

"We are delighted. Now I must present you to my mother, to the grandmother of Marie-Josephe." He turned to an old lady and spoke rapidly in French. He said to Jim with a shrug. "You must understand, alas, that my mother has no English. No word at all. *Maman, je vous présente Monsieur Carver, soldat anglais, ami de la famille.*"

Jim found himself looking at an elderly edition of Marie-Josephe. The resemblance was so startling that he blinked. True it was that her face was a maze of wrinkles, while Marie-Josephe's skin was as smooth as ivory. But in spite of that, the delicate bone formation was exactly the same and the eyes were as bright as those of her granddaughter. He smiled involuntarily, and the old lady, as if she had divined his thought, smiled back. He took her brown hand in his and, to his astonishment, he bent over it and kissed it lightly. 'My God,' he thought, 'what the hell are you doing, Jim Carver? Have you gone stark, staring mad, kissing women's hands? Thank God, the men from the Darts Club aren't here to see you. . . .' He straightened his back. The old lady, her dark eyes frighteningly observant, was still smiling at him. She said briefly to her son:

"*Monsieur est un chevalier.*"

"My grandmother says that you are a . . . a *chevalier*. I don't know the word in English. It means that she considers you to be noble and that she likes you. It is most rare! And now come. This is my fiancé, Henri Dubot."

So this was the man Marie-Josephe was going to marry, this was the man whose children she would one day bear. Henri was about thirty, and already showing the first indications of the plumpness he would acquire with the years. He was undeniably good-looking, in a dark, rather hirsute way, and his skin had a paleness about it as if he worked too long indoors. His mouth, under a neat moustache, was full and mobile, and he was quick to smile. He was dressed in a black coat and waistcoat and striped trousers, and his linen was immaculate. He looked what he was, a successful and confident man whose feet were firmly on the earth—and that was where he proposed to keep them. Marie-Josephe said solemnly:

"This will be a good occasion for you to speak English, Henri. For many months my fiancé has been to a school for English in Boulogne, Jim, and sometimes I talk with him to practise. Now it is the big moment!"

Henri Dubot laughed with a flash of white teeth. He said, speaking very slowly and precisely, having a little trouble with his aspirates:

"I am very 'appy to meet you, Sir. It is a pleasure for me." He turned to Marie-Josephe. "*Voila, chérie!*" He kissed her lightly on both cheeks, and put his arm with an oddly possessive gesture around her shoulders. "You will see, *chérie,* that I have not wasted my time."

Madame Berthier said carefully:

"We have not begun to have lunch yet, Monsieur. . . ."

"My name is Jim. Just Jim."

". . . Monsieur Jim. We were waiting for Marie-Josephe. While my daughter is preparing for you a place at our table, you would like to drink a small *apéritif,* a glass perhaps of Calvados?" She turned to her husband. "Louis, our guest would take a glass of Calvados with us. Marie-Josephe, please to make ready a place, while Papa gives *un apéritif.*"

"Volontiers, Maman."

She slid easily and swiftly from her fiancé's arm and walked towards the door that led to the kitchen. Jim watched her go. Never in his life had he known anyone to walk with such dignity and with such an air of being alone.

He stood by the porcelain stove, facing Henri Dubot. Marie-Josephe, her father and mother had left the room. There were long pauses between sentences, and Jim could almost see the process of word-building going on in Henri Dubot's mind. He only spoke when he had picked each unfamiliar word out of his vocabulary and attached it to another word and formed a sentence, complete with commas and full stops. Then he produced it with great care, as a single, solitary, perfect unit, bearing no relationship to what had gone before or to what was likely to come after.

"You were a soldier in the British Army, Sir?"

"Yes. That's right. I was in the 25th Lancers, in tanks. You know, tanks. But you mustn't call me 'sir'."

There was a long pause.

"You like very much to come to France, to Boulogne?"

"Yes. Very much. But I'm only here for the day. I go back tonight."

On a ledge over the stove there were two highly polished shell-cases of the 1914–1918 war. They were brass and came from a French ·75. Damn good gun it was, too. Not up to our 25-pounders, but a damn good gun, all the same.

"England is a monarchy while France is a Republic," said Henri Dubot portentously. "Each system has much to recommend it."

"Yes, I've . . . I've often thought that," said Jim. "We like our Royal Family very much in England."

"They are also much loved in France, Monsieur."

There was a photograph on the piano of a little girl in a white dress. She had on her face a look of most unnatural piety, and she clasped a Missal with self-consciously reverent fingers. Jim had seen photographs like that before in French houses, and he knew, without even looking any more, that it was of Marie-Josephe on the occasion of her first Communion.

"The French are a gay people, given to light wines and to dancing," said Henri Dubot. "The English prefer beer and football."

"Yes," said Jim. "Of course in the summer you do bicycle-racing and we play cricket."

"Ah! Cricket. I 'ave 'eard of this exciting cricket."

Jim looked desperately towards the door of the kitchen. If only Marie-Josephe would come back, or her father, or somebody. He glanced again at the piano, at the photograph and, as he looked back, he caught Marie-Josephe's grandmother's eye. She was looking at him, her dark eyes—Marie-Josephe's eyes—fixed on his face in a shrewd, unblinking gaze. So intense, so searching was that look that Jim shifted his feet. Then a strange thing happened. The maze of wrinkles dissolved into the smile of a young girl, and a gleam of pure malice shone momentarily in her eyes—and Jim knew with certainty that that malice was not directed towards him. He smiled at the old lady. He was glad that he had kissed her hand.

"I 'ad some friends in the British Army 'oo, I am sure, played at cricket. I was the friend of many officers, of Brigadiers, Colonels, Majors—all cricketers. I also was acquainted with a Captain, a Captain 'oo's name was Edwards. 'E was a merry fellow."

"I don't think I knew him. You see, I was a sergeant."

"Please?"

"A sergeant." He traced the outlines of three imaginary stripes on his arm. "I was a sergeant."

"You were not officer?"

"No. An N.C.O. A sergeant."

Henri Dubot raised his eyebrows. Happy in the knowledge that he had a silent ally in the room, Jim suppressed an inward giggle. He was aware that he had been dismissed as a person of no consequence.

"Fall out the N.C.O.'s."

He turned as the kitchen door opened and Marie-Josephe came into the room. It seemed that with her came all the sunshine of France.

The Calvados was colourless and it was offered wtih great formality in glasses that were no bigger than thimbles. Everybody said *'Santé'* to each other, and Jim swallowed his at a gulp. What it lacked in quantity it certainly had in power—for the drink went down his throat like red-hot barbed wire and twisted itself into a knot in the membrane of his stomach. He put down the glass with a cough and felt in his pocket for a handkerchief. Just as he realised with embarrassment that he had come without one, Marie-Josephe slid her own into his hand and he took it gratefully. He thought that no one had seen her swift, covert gesture, but he was wrong. He cleared his throat and put the handkerchief carefully into his breast pocket. He'd return it to her later—or not. He would very much like to have something tangible, something that he could hold in his hand when he would think, in times to come, of this extraordinary, enchanted day.

He sat between Madame Berthier and Marie-Josephe. Next to her, on her right, was Henri Dubot, and her grandmother sat opposite him, her son on her right. Marie-Josephe, during her ten minutes' absence in the kitchen, had made a *quiche aux champignons,* a sort of deep flan of scrambled eggs and chopped mushrooms, and she asked Jim if he liked it. He said that it was jolly good.

"I am not a woman given to exaggeration," said Marie-Josephe, "but I hope that you consider me to be a good cook."

"I think you are a marvellous cook."

Henri Dubot removed the napkin from inside his collar and wiped his mouth. It was manifest that the process of verbal brick-laying had started again and the table waited for the pronouncement. He beamed at Marie-Josephe.

"I am in accord with the Sergeant. After we have been married, you will always prepare *quiche aux champignons* for *déjeuner* on Sundays."

It was not only a command. The words had been carefully chosen to achieve more than one purpose, and Jim, his ears and his mind attuned to a new sensitivity, read their several messages. Monsieur Dubot had deliberately used the word 'Sergeant'. That had been done to establish Jim once again and even more firmly as a non-commissioned officer. "After we have been married." That phrase too was more than a gentle reminder of his status as the future bridegroom of . . . a marvellous cook. His bride had been relegated to the kitchen and she had her orders. On week-days she would presumably be free to make suggestions, but for Sundays the master had stated his wishes, and it would be Marie-Josephe's duty to see that they were carried out. Yet all these subtleties faded before one shining truth: Monsieur Dubot had considered it necessary to issue this many-pronged challenge and, because of that, Jim was deeply content.

It was left to Grandmère Berthier to electrify the table. Her dark eyes flashed and she chuckled. She said in fluent English that had in it the bewildering faint cadence of an Irish brogue:

"There are times in the year when you can get neither eggs nor mushrooms, Henri."

Where? How? When?

While her astonished family plied her with questions, Grandmère Berthier sat back and refused to be drawn. Yes, it was true that she had *quelques mots,* a few words of English. She had learned them a long time ago, it must be many years now. It was a matter of no importance, and there were things of far greater interest to discuss than the vocabulary of an old lady. The recent election, for example, the mounting price of butter, the quality of the new wine. The family had a guest at their table, and it was to him that their conversation should be addressed. She said suddenly, sharply, to her son, *"Je t'en prie, Louis."* The subject was closed.

The flan was followed by *rôti de bœuf,* served generously. It was beef such as Jim had not eaten since before the war and, no economist, he marvelled at the bare butchers' shops of England. *Petits pois,* cooked in butter, *sauté* potatoes, salad, Camembert, fruit—this was the most delicious lunch he had eaten for years. It was with a sense of genial repletion that he noticed Monsieur Dubot's air of preoccupation. Something was coming. With mathematical precision the cartridge was slid into the breech, the bolt was shut, the rifle was raised, the sights aligned, first pressure taken on the trigger. Now for it. . . .

"It was the English," said Monsieur Dubot in accusing tones, "who burned Joan of Arc in the year 1431."

"And it was the same English," said Marie-Josephe gently, "who came to France in 1944 and who now lie beside my brother Denis in the *Cimetière de l'Est.*" She stood up. "I would like your permission, Papa, to show Jim the farm."

"With pleasure, Marie-Josephe. My daughter, Monsieur, is a friend to each of the animals."

"You desire me to accompany you, *chérie*?" asked Monsieur Dubot anxiously.

"As you wish, Henri. But I know how you care for your coffee and liqueur and your cigar. Also, there is the question of Siki. And Jim, I remember, does not take coffee. Do you, Jim?"

"Never," said Jim. He coughed. "At least, practically never."

"You will return soon, please. It is necessary for me to return to Boulogne this afternoon, *chérie*. I have a conference with a client at 'alf-past three."

"Oh yes," said Marie-Josephe soothingly, "we will return. Come, Jim."

As he left the dining-room, Jim glanced involuntarily at Grandmère Berthier. Was there, or was there not, the same gleam of sardonic satisfaction in her dark, unfathomable eyes? He half bowed to her, and she smiled.

Yes, there was.

CHAPTER TEN

"FUNNY thing," said Mr. Collins, as he swallowed the last of the Yorkshire pudding and put down his knife and fork, "funny thing. I wonder what can have happened to Jim Carver. He said to me, leaving the ship, that he had a bit of private business to attend to, and that he'd come straight on here for his dinner. Well, I'm the last person in the world to enquire into anybody's private business, but I can't help wondering if he's all right. Do you think he's all right, Mr. Grenfell?"

"I *know* he's all right."

"Oh, you do, do you?" Mr. Collins raised his eyebrows. "All he said to me was that he had a bit of private business to do and, as you very well know, Mr. Grenfell, I'd rather tear my tongue out than enquire into what other people don't want to tell me freely and of their own accord. On the other hand, I am the Secretary of the Darts Club Outing—honorary secretary, I need hardly say—and as such——" He paused expectantly.

Luke said soothingly:

"I shouldn't worry at all. He'll turn up all right."

"I sincerely hope so. This Outing has been a great responsibility." The treacle-tart was brought in and he attacked it with gusto. "A great responsibility. This isn't England, Mr. Grenfell, and the people's ways are not English ways—and I'd be sorry indeed if Jim got himself mixed up with the Frenchies. You don't think he has, do you, Mr. Grenfell?"

"People have in the past, you know—and without doing themselves any irreparable harm. Think of Henry the Fifth and his Kate."

"In the past, I dare say; not that I can recollect the lady you mention. But this isn't the past. It's the present." To give emphasis to this weighty pronouncement, he repeated it. "It's the present." He went on with his treacle-tart, occasionally glancing at a slip of paper from his waistcoat pocket. His big moment was almost at hand, the moment for which he had practised so often before the bedroom looking-glass. At long last, the remnants of the treacle-tart were removed, the waitress ordered out of the room and the doors shut.

Mr. Collins rose. He surveyed the members of The Hand and Flower Darts Club with authoritative benevolence, and conversation was stilled. He blew his nose and put his finger-tips on the edge of the table.

"Gentlemen," he said, "far away from home as we are, I ask you to charge your glasses and to drink to the health of Her Majesty, the Queen. Stand up, Charley."

The loyal toast was drunk and, as Shorty stubbed out the butt of his fifth cigarette, Mr. Collins added malevolently, "Gentlemen, you may smoke."

Again he surveyed the room, putting his thumbs in the armholes of his waistcoat and rocking gently.

"Now, Gentlemen, I won't detain you long, but I have got one or two things to say. We have had, by and large, a most successful season—with one or two exceptions. In the match against our friends of the Trout and Pike, we were left with thirty-five to get, five and double fifteen. Now that was a little problem that should have presented no difficulties to gentlemen of your calibre. . . ."

As Mr. Collins picked his way unerringly through a maze of long-forgotten scores and subtractions, the members of The Hand and Flower Darts Club thought their own thoughts.

They had plenty of time for thinking. It was a quarter-past two before his dreary monologue came to an end and The Hand and Flower Darts Club was once more temporarily united in relief.

"Now, Gentlemen, as we all know, the boat sails at ten minutes past six. It may be that you gentlemen might like to have a look at the shops, or you might like to have a run out to Wimmeroo, which is a select little resort about three miles away. I am sorry that our good friend Jim Carver hasn't turned up yet, but that—I'm sure you'll all agree—is his misfortune. Whatever you do decide to do, the great thing is to stick together. Suppose you do get separated—and I most sincerely hope you won't—we all meet here, come what may, at five o'clock precisely. As for myself, I have a little commission to execute for Mrs. Collins, so I shall not be accompanying you. And now, Gentlemen, as they say here, 'oh revoor' and keep yourselves to yourselves. Gentlemen, I thank you."

Mr. Collins sat down. He was a little disappointed that there was no round of applause. He frowned in some displeasure, as Trevor Hilgrove rose to his feet. Trevor's manner was easy and beguiling.

"My good friends," he said, "as a non-member of your Club, it is perhaps a presumption on my part to address you. On the other hand, I have been fascinated by the many mathematical post-mortems conducted with uncanny skill by Mr. Collins, and I congratulate him whole-heartedly on an elephantine memory. Like our friend Jim Carver and the Master of Ceremonies himself"—he bowed towards Mr. Collins—"I too have a personal errand in Boulogne. It is a duty rather than a pleasure and concerns a sick friend. May I suggest therefore that those of us who wish to stick together should do so, and that others should be permitted to go their diverse ways?"

This time the applause was immediate and hearty. Before it had subsided, Charley Brewer was on his feet. His speech was brief and to the point.

" 'Ere, 'ere," said Charley.

Before The Hand and Flower Darts Club was half-way up the hill between the port and the Old Town, it was no longer a single unit. Charley Brewer was the first to detach himself.

While his companions were looking with glazed and incredulous eyes at the shop windows, a special sort of merchandise had caught Charley's eye and he crossed the road to inspect it more closely. It hung on a pole outside a combined drapers and toyshop. It was a pair of old-fashioned, lace-up pink stays, its four elastic suspenders fluttering in the frolic wind that came off the sea. Charley looked at it for a long time, fingering the bundle of francs in his pocket. Then he stood on tiptoe and reached up and gave one of the suspenders a playful tug. The door of the shop was flung open and the proprietor, a red-faced man in his shirt-sleeves, shot out. He jerked his face to within one inch of Charley's and hissed out a stream of what Charley could only suppose to be invective. The word '*salle-oh*' was repeated several times on a rising crescendo. Discretion was clearly the better part of valour, and Charley whipped off his bowler and tucked it under his arm and his white gym shoes went twinkling down the street and round the corner. By the time he considered it safe to draw up, he was in a sort of strange market-place, entirely surrounded by French people, and at least temporarily lost to Mr. Collins and to his friends and colleagues of The Hand and Flower Darts Club.

High time, too. . . .

Trevor Hilgrove had not been in Boulogne since before the war, and he was uncertain as to how to reach the *Café Gérard,* so what could be more natural than that he should ask a policeman? It gave him a certain sense of satisfaction to invoke the assistance of the law in finding the place he had chosen for his proposed activities, and he thanked the policeman with almost exaggerated courtesy. His way lay through mean streets, and though one side of the *place Robespierre* had suffered in the bombardment, the *Café Gérard* had remained unscathed. Trevor gaily walked between the twin bay trees in their green pots and pushed his way through the revolving glass door.

The café was crowded and noisy, for here was Boulogne's Sunday afternoon meeting-place. An electric-fan spun lazily from the ceiling, churning the eternal sour smell of cigarettes, sweat, concrete and *Eau de Javel.* Behind the bar with its beer handles and its coffee machine, sat Madame, her onyx eyes darting for ever from customer to customer. Dogs ran under the tables, sniffing and yapping, getting in the way of scurrying waitresses with their laden trays, barking at the children who chattered round the door. In one corner, a pontifical group of business-men played *Belotte* with great solemnity, and between the tables an olive-skinned Algerian, in a fez, burnous and sandals, obsequiously offered lengths of silk and rugs and rings to the housewives of Boulogne.

For a moment Trevor Hilgrove stood by the door, taking in every detail of the seething activity. He noted the swing door marked 'TOILETTES et TELEPHONE' and the notice that said 'ENGLISH SPOKEN: WELSH RABBIT: STEAK AND SHIPS'. The clock behind the bar struck three, and Trevor stood to one side as the revolving door turned slowly to admit yet another customer.

Punctual as ever—that was Pierre!

The new-comer looked casually round the café, chose the only table that had two vacant chairs, made his way to it, sat down, putting his elbows on his despatch-case. Equally casually, Trevor followed him and took the chair opposite, leaning his dart-board against the leg of the table. Neither gave the slightest sign of recognition. Pierre was a man of about thirty. He wore a beret and a long, light jacket cut in the style known as American drape. His crêpe-soled shoes were elaborately brogued, and light yellow in colour, with triangular brass lace-holes. His hair, under his slanting beret, was longer than most and he needed a shave. He ordered a coffee and a *fine,* while Trevor ordered a glass of beer. Pierre stroked his unshaven chin and took a copy of *Combat* from his despatch-case and began to read. Not to be outdone, Trevor took his folded *News of the World* from his pocket and busied himself with the front page.

Seemingly oblivious of each other's presence, the two confederates waited with every manifestation of innocent detachment for 'Operation Timepiece' to begin.

It was purely accidental that Luke Grenfell found himself walking up the hill in close proximity to Shorty—who ran for Mr. McIsaac the bookie. During Mr. Collins's interminable speech he had once or twice had forced upon his consciousness the fact that Shorty was staring at him through slitted eyes, as if trying to concentrate upon him all the malevolence of which he was capable. Luke had shifted uncomfortably. An initial sense of embarrassment had changed to one of sharp irritation. He had always known that Shorty didn't like him, and sometimes he had vaguely wondered what he had done, what mistake he had made, whereby he had engendered the hatred of this unhappy introvert with built-up shoulders and high heels. Over a period of time the dislike had become mutual, and Luke had simply given up trying. Just as Shorty had no time for him, he had no time for Shorty. Now a curious thought struck him. Why had Jim Carver asked him if Shorty knew he had been a rating in the Navy? Could that have anything to do with Shorty's wholly inexplicable attitude? Was it worth having one more final crack at trying to find out the cause of his implacable enmity? Luke decided not. Let the silly little spiv go on his own tortured way. Shorty was only a yard or two on his right and Luke instinctively increased the distance between them. Shorty looked round.

"All right," he said, "all right. I ain't got fleas."

Luke stopped. He took off his horn-rimmed spectacles and

polished them furiously. Then he strode after Shorty and put his hand on one built-up shoulder and swung Shorty round. In spite of his stoop, Luke towered over him. He said angrily:

"I don't know whether you've got fleas or not. I know you've got something and I also know that you're bloody rude."

Shorty's eyes widened. This was a new Mr. Grenfell. This tall man with the set face had nothing to do with the genial, contemptible dispenser of free pints in the public bar of The Hand and Flower. Two courses were open to him. The first was to upper-cut Mr. Grenfell slap-bang on the point of the chin, the other was . . . well the other. Shorty chose the other. He shook his head, grinning feebly:

"Langwidge, Mr. Grenfell."

Luke dropped his hand off Shorty's shoulder. He said in disgust:

"You make me sick."

"You don't make me feel too good myself."

"Oh, go to hell. You're just a waste of time."

Luke turned away and began to walk up the hill. The incident had barely lasted thirty seconds, but now that it was over, his muscles were quivering. He walked quickly, looking neither to the right nor to the left, waiting for his anger to subside. The brightness of the day was like a benediction, and it was not long before he was able to divert his thoughts into more agreeable channels. A row with Shorty had obviously been boiling up for some time. Well, now it was over. For a few brief hours he was in the France he loved, and he desired ardently to savour it to the full. The senses of the majority of people, he supposed, were stimulated by the images of the eye, those of some by sound, by remembered words or by remembered music, by touch or by taste. For him, smell was the most evocative of the senses, and now, on this shining day, he perceived France most keenly and acutely through his nostrils. He stopped outside a café. The smell of coffee and bread and garlic and wine tangled itself in the salt smell of the sea, and he breathed deeply. To hell with Shorty. . . .

"Mr. Grenfell."

"Oh, my God! You again. What do you want now?"

Shorty said truculently:

"What Jim Carver said, is it true?"

"I have no way of knowing what Jim Carver said."

"Jim Carver said that in the war you was a sailor, on the lower deck, he said, and that you had to swim for it twice."

"Well, what of it?"

Shorty shuffled his feet and put his hands in his pockets and took them out again. His ghastly shoes did the steps of a little hornpipe on the pavement and then stopped. After a long pause he said carelessly, looking away across the street:

"My Dad was a sailor."

The smell of the café was pungent in Luke's nostrils. He took off his spectacles and polished them, slowly this time. He said in a not unfriendly voice:

"Care for a drink, Shorty?"

"I don't mind if I do."

Fred Collins was having a very trying afternoon. He flattered himself that his after-dinner speech had been a considerable success and that the boys had given him their undivided attention, but he had hoped that they would have wanted to stick together. And then there was Jim Carver. Jim hadn't even turned up at all—and no one had set eyes on him since the boat docked. Private bit of business indeed! And where was Charley Brewer? Mr. Collins had seen him crossing the road ten minutes back, and then, a minute or two after, he'd seen someone in white gym shoes going down the street like a bat out of hell. Mr. Collins told himself again and again that the fugitive *couldn't* have been Charley, but the awful, nagging suspicion remained that it *had* been none other than the Captain of The Hand and Flower Darts Club in headlong flight.

Mr. Hilgrove presumably had gone off to see his sick friend. At least he'd shown himself gentlemanly and asked permission to go. . . . Even Mr. Grenfell was nowhere to be seen. One minute he'd been arguing with Shorty only a yard or two away, and somehow they must have gone off separately, for there was no sign of Mr. Grenfell, or of Shorty either. Net result was that here stood Mr. Fred Collins, Licensee of The Hand and Flower, Honorary Secretary and Treasurer of the Darts Club, Honorary Organiser and Treasurer of the Outing, alone in Boulogne, without knowing what any of them were up to. It's not that he asked for gratitude, but only for fair play.

Now what was it Emma had reminded him to get? A pair

of nylons, size ten and a half, and a nice beige. Trouble was, where to get 'em. He walked along the *rue Victor Hugo*, looking in all the shop windows. Almost immediately he found what he wanted. It was a shop called *'Lili de Paris'*. Carefully looking round to make sure he was unobserved by any of his errant companions, Mr. Collins looked in the window.

A trio of waxen ladies, each wearing two wisps of black chiffon in the appropriate places, struck seductive attitudes against a painted Riviera sunset. On the left, a single, amputated, silk-stockinged glass leg bore a ticket saying: "*Demandez la marque 'SEXY'*"—and more important than any of these things was the discreet notice on the right—ENGLISH SPOKEN. Though there was little resemblance between the glass leg and the living limbs of Mrs. Collins, this was obviously the place. Scenting trade, Lili herself had come to the door of the shop and had opened it invitingly. She was a suave, sophisticated young woman who looked as if she had been poured out of a jug into her black satin frock and remembered to say 'when' at exactly the right moment. She had patent-leather hair, dark blue shadows under her eyes, lashes like dung-forks and a purple mouth. She gave Mr. Collins a brief, painted smile.

"*Vous désirez, Monsieur?*"

"Speak English?"

"Oh yes," said Lili, "yes please."

"Got any nylons, size ten and a half, and a nice beige?"

Lili drew to one side. She said simply:

"*Entrez, Monsieur.*"

Feeling rather like a man who has rashly accepted an invitation to supper with Lucrezia Borgia, Mr. Collins gave a furtive glance to the right and to the left, and stepped into the shop's dim interior.

It seemed that Lili's claim to a knowledge of English must have been exaggerated, or Mr. Collins's requirements misunderstood, for after five minutes had passed the glass panel at the back of the window slid back. Smiling slightly, Lili insinuated her filleted person into the window, removed all the chiffon from one of the wax models and disappeared again into the shop. A further five minutes passed before Mr. Collins emerged. He was carrying a neat little parcel tied up with coloured string, his roll of franc notes had been considerably depleted, and he still needed a pair of nylons, size ten and a half and a nice beige.

In spite of that, he had encountered the French and remained reasonably unscathed. Greatly emboldened by his escape, he strode along the *rue Victor Hugo* with a new confidence, a new buoyancy. He even began to whistle the opening bars of "*As I walk along the Bois de Boulogne with an independent air* . . ." His steps led him in the direction of the harbour, that ever-present link with the Homeland. In the devastation of broken houses, one row alone had remained more or less intact. It contained a ship-chandlers, an antique shop, a bicycle shop and a café. As Mr. Collins passed the café, a surge of tinny music smote his ears, and he stopped in his tracks. He listened entranced to the song that reverberated out of the horn of an ancient gramophone—for it took him back more than thirty-five years, away from the mud and blood of the Somme to the first night of his first leave in London, with Zeppelins sailing over Piccadilly and a girl in an electric-blue frock singing:

"You called me Baby Doll a year ago,
You told me I was very nice to know. . . ."

A woman stood at the door of the café. Even to Mr. Collins's unselective eye she was not a very attractive woman, for her face was a mask of paint, she wore glass ear-rings that hung to her shoulders, and her age was nearer sixty than fifty. She gave him a smile of infinite languor.

"Allo, you old son-of-a-gun."

"Hullo," said the Licensee of The Hand and Flower.

CHAPTER ELEVEN

ONCE again Jim followed Marie-Josephe along the cool passage and out into the day. The sunshine was white and dazzling. A few chickens picked in the shade of an old farm-cart resting on its shafts alongside the wall of a barn with a roof of golden tiles. In the quiet afternoon there was the continuous hum of flies over the redolent muck-heap and the soft clucking of the chickens. Marie-Josephe crossed the yard and took Siki off his chain. Having reassured himself that this was indeed the same man to whom he had been introduced, Siki wagged his tail. Marie-Josephe said happily:

"You see, he has not forgotten you. I told you that he has given you the freedom of *Clos d'Argent*, and it is so. But only during the day. Now tell me, do you know anything about calves?"

Jim checked a smile. He said humbly, "I'm always ready to learn."

"I will teach you. Siki, *attends moi*."

She led the way to a stable and unbolted the door. When his eyes were accustomed to the dimness, Jim saw three very small calves standing almost knee-deep in straw. They crowded together on their spindly legs, blinking and twitching their tails. One of them was black and white, and the others tawny. Marie-Josephe walked slowly towards the group and put out her hand. One of the tawny calves, after a preliminary sniff, sucked her fingers, and she scratched its head with her left hand, talking to it with a soft, soothing voice. Jim leaned against the door of the stable, watching her. It was a pleasant thing for him to see, and he felt that he had known Marie-Josephe for a very long time. She caught his eye and smiled.

"Each has her name. This one is *Petite Etoile*, which is 'Small Star', and this one is *Espoir du Matin*, 'Hope of the Morning'. The smallest one has not yet a name. All are *génisses*. I don't know the English word. It means they are all *jeunes filles*, young ladies."

"Heifers."

"Yes, that is the word. All are heifers. It is very lucky to have heifers. Now would you like to see the father of these two, of *Petite Etoile* and *Espoir*? He is a boule."

"A what?"

"A boule."

"Oh! A bull." Jim laughed. He said, "Say 'bull'."

"Boule."

"No. Not like that. B-U-L-L. Bull!"

"Boule. No." She shook her head. "It is impossible for me to say it."

"Try once more. Say 'bull'."

"Bul."

He laughed. "It's no use, Marie-Josephe. Let him remain a 'boule'. Now, may I see him?"

"Yes, but not to touch. His name is *Prince des Etoiles,* which is a very grand name and means 'Prince of the Stars'. He is like Siki, very angry with people he does not know, and it would take a long time for him to be your friend. You have so little time. It is very sad."

So little time. . . .

It was with a sense of amazement that Jim realised that only that morning he had been in London. It seemed to him that an eternity of time had passed since his feet had been on the pavements of Saint John's Wood, that his lungs had breathed the air of North-west Eight, and that he had heard the bells of Saint Saviour's. But it had been that very morning. Only a few hours ago he had seen his companions of The Hand and Flower Darts Club clearly, but now a grey veil seemed to come between him and their faces. He even had difficulty in remembering their names—Mr. Collins and Charley . . . Shorty and Luke Grenfell with the horn-rimmed spectacles. . . . So completely had he entered this strange and unfamiliar world, so utterly was he one with this half-forgotten, sharply-remembered girl, that everything else was out of focus. The edges of the past were blurred and only the present was real. And yet there was a contradiction, an acceleration in the passage of time, for now the minutes were racing away in headlong flight. He was dismayed by the brevity of the space left to him, dismayed and bewildered that it was beyond human power to check, even for one enchanted minute, the awful gallop of the hours.

"This is *Prince des Etoiles.*"

As the top of the slotted half-door of the loose-box opened, an enormous bull turned his head slowly and looked at them.

He was ringed and had a thick cluster of curls on his forehead. Like that of his daughters, his skin was tawny and shone like silk. Marie-Josephe said:

"Do you like him?"

He looked the bull over carefully before replying. His answer was considered and truthful:

"He's not bad. Not bad at all. A little heavy on the shoulder, I'd say, but he's well sprung with plenty of heart room. How old is he? Three, three and a half?"

"He is three years and two months." She faced him, her eyes puzzled. "But you said to me that you wished to learn about such things. I believe that you mock yourself of me. You did not say that you knew."

He looked at the bull again, at the gigantic head and wicked, pink-rimmed eyes.

"Do you go into that box with him?"

"Sometimes. But I always wear the same coat when I do. I think that he knows my coat and the . . . the odour of my coat more than he knows me. It is not very flattering. Boules are like that. My father has said these days that I must not go in, but we are friends, this boule and I."

"Your father is quite right." He saw the bull's head begin to lower and she shut the top of the half-door and bolted it. He swung round on his heel. He said to her, very seriously:

"Marie-Josephe, will you make me a promise?"

Startled by his suddenly unsmiling face, she fell back a step.

"What is this promise?"

"That you will never in your life go into that box again alone—or with anybody else, either. And if you take him out, take him on a spreader."

"A 'spreader'. What is this thing, a 'spreader'?"

"A pole with a clip on it that snaps into the ring. You could never hold him with a rope."

"Ah. A 'spreader'. I had forgotten the word, but I know it quite well. Yes, I will promise you."

"Seriously. I'm terribly in earnest."

She was very happy that he should be so anxious for her safety. She said:

"I promise."

"Good. At that age, bulls can be damn dangerous. You won't forget?"

"I won't forget. You may trust me absolutely."

"I do." He gave a deep sigh. "That's better. Now what am I to see?"

"What would you like to see?"

"I don't mind. I want to be with you, Marie-Josephe."

"Do you? I am very glad."

He looked at her, frowning. He knew very clearly the thought he wanted to express, but he found difficulty in clothing it with words.

"It's very queer."

"What's very queer?"

"You are. You are so many different people. I had always thought of you as a little girl, and the first shock I had was when I saw you weren't a little girl any more. When you spoke to me in the *Cimetière de l'Est* you knocked the breath out of me. Since then I've seen you in a number of rôles, driving a car, being a marvellous cook, being . . . somebody's fiancée, and now I see you talking to calves and being an ass about . . . about 'boules'. Which is the real Marie-Josephe?"

She looked at him steadily.

"And you, Jim, have not changed at all. Not in any way. That is why it is a great joy to have you here."

"It is a great joy for me to be here. But you haven't answered my question. Who is the real Marie-Josephe?"

Who was the real Marie-Josephe?

Up to this morning, up to less than two hours ago, she thought she had known. There had been little enough to know. She darted back across the years, and saw the safe and simple scenes of her childhood pass in swift succession. She saw puppy fat emerging into firm flesh, pinafores becoming frocks, socks becoming stockings, sandals become shoes, *toi* becoming *vous*. These changes and a thousand others had happened to her, and she had accepted all of them calmly, aware of, without being awake to, her mounting maturity. Only one thing had happened to disrupt the tranquil rhythm of her girlhood.

The man who stood beside her now had first entered her life in strange guise. He had not been a man at all, but Saint George of England, Saint George in a black beret, Saint George stripped to his sunburned waist, Saint George clattering into her father's orchard in the turret of a Comet tank, Saint George's hand on the barrel of a 77-millimetre gun.

She had included him and his crew in her prayers. . . . Nobby his wireless operator, Mike his gunner, Mac his driver. But then, as the symbolic Saint George had turned into the living Sergeant Jim, the man who helped her to wash the separator in the dairy, the man to whom she sang *'Savez-vous planter les choux'*, she had dropped Nobby and Mike and Mac from her supplications, and Jim had become the sole beneficiary.

She had begun to be in the state of being in love with him because he was an idea. She had gone on to love him with all the inarticulate ardour of an adolescent girl because he was brave and gentle and strong. Then he had gone away. She had hidden herself in an apple tree the day the Lancers had clattered out of her father's freed fields towards the final battles, and watched through the leaves as the tanks took to the roads in dust and thunder. When they had gone she had climbed down and slowly traced, with her sandalled foot, the bite of their tracks in the grass. It had been a long time before that first tempestuous emotion had died, a long time before her life sank back into its even pattern.

She had met Henri Dubot. At first she had been amused and not a little flattered by his interest in her. Seeing the possibility of a suitable union, Grandmère Berthier had entered the lists on her granddaughter's behalf. Her influence was decisive, and it was not long before Marie-Josephe was showing Henri's ring to her friends and, somewhat dazedly, receiving their congratulations on a most satisfactory engagement. Henri Dubot was a man of dignity and stature, and it would be, in the material sense, a very good marriage. Once she had got used to the idea, she had been well content to envisage the solid domesticity that lay so securely before her. Soon she would be this man's wife, and the identity of Mademoiselle Marie-Josephe would be submerged in that of Madame Henri Dubot. She had been discreetly instructed by her mother, and she had hoped that, in the fullness of time, she would bear Henri children. That was the purpose behind the blossoming of her breasts and the deepening of her loins. The roar of centuries told her clearly that this was so. Church and State echoed the verdict. She had therefore accepted the future of marriage with equanimity, and had considered herself to be reasonably knowledgeable. She had rejected and run away from the most tentative pre-nuptial advances of her fiancé. Once *Monsieur le Curé* had pronounced his blessing, she would have this traditional submission to make, this age-old duty to perform. But until that time she wished to remain untouched and remote from the hands of men.

She looked at Jim Carver, and she knew with bewilderment and alarm that her mother's words had meant less than nothing. One might as well try to describe the quality of colour to a blind child as to seek to clothe in words something so personal and so intimate. She had wished to bear children without having the faintest glimmer of the import of their creation. Now, in the presence of an English sergeant, she was aware of a new thought. It had come unbidden, and it stayed to confuse her. She had accepted the prospect of marriage as she accepted dawn and dusk and the germination of seed. But could it not be that the secondary and more subtle purpose of her receptive body was to dispel the last barrier between a man and a woman in love so that together they could know a physical and a spiritual harmony that would uplift and transport them to the very Feet of God?

It was a strange, unlikely instrument that Providence had chosen to stir the fire that had smouldered over the years in the caves of her heart. It was the severed cable of a starter motor. In seeing the work of this man's hands, the man himself had been revealed to her, in his strength, in his simplicity, in his power to heal.

"Come back, Marie-Josephe. You've been a million miles away."

She shook her head. But it was true. In the space of a few seconds she had travelled a very long way away and entered realms hitherto unknown. Now she was back, and she was a living girl whose movements she controlled with her mind and her brain. She saw Henri Dubot as a shadow seen through gauze. She saw Jim Carver clearly as the man she loved and had always loved. She looked at him without faltering.

"You ask me—who is the real Marie-Josephe? I know now. And I think . . . I think you may know too before you return to England."

It seemed for a moment that Jim could not have heard her soft reply, for his fingers went on beating a little uninterrupted tattoo on the half-door. Then all of a sudden his fingers were motionless. The hens still clucked and picked in the shadow under the farm-cart, the hum of flies was a continuous sound in the warm afternoon. Everything was the same and yet everything had changed. It was from a great distance that he heard a man's voice calling.

"Marie-Josephe."

She started and turned and faced the house. Henri Dubot was standing at the door, his hands cupped to his mouth. He called out something, but she couldn't hear the words. She said, "I can't hear. Come and tell me."

"Me? Come to you. Oh no." He smiled and pointed. "It is better that I rest 'ere. Regard, please, Siki."

The dog was crouched flat against the ground, one wet lip lifted. Marie-Josephe glanced at him and smiled. She called across the yard:

"I am sorry. I forgot that you and Siki are not great friends. Jim, please put Siki on his chain."

"Do you really want me to?"

"Yes. I do. Please."

"Good. This is where I press on regardless and start being Daniel again."

He walked confidently to the dog, rubbed his head and led him to the outhouse by his collar. Clipped on his chain. Henri Dubot advanced cautiously. He said, smiling:

"You are one of courage, my dear fellow. As for me, I detest that animal there. But detest. Marie-Josephe, your grandmother wishes to speak with you. She 'as gone to 'er room."

"I will go to her at once."

"Per'aps the Sergeant will like to take a liqueur with me, yes? We will wait together for Marie-Josephe and 'ave a nice conversation in English."

"Yes, indeed. Thanks very much."

They walked side by side along the passage. Marie-Josephe had gone on ahead, and Jim could hear her footsteps on the stairs. Henri Dubot poured out two tiny glasses of Benedictine and presented one with a bow.

"Well, cheerio. That is what I learn from my friend, Captain Edwards, to say always 'cheerio'."

"Cheerio."

Henri Dubot sat down and carefully adjusted the crease in his trousers. He said with great precision:

"Marie-Josephe relates to me that you also are fiancé, that soon you will marry an English lady."

Jim looked at him sharply. He was smiling with every manifestation of friendly interest. Jim put down his glass. He was suddenly very tired. The heat had all of an instant been drained from the sun and the colour from the day. He said slowly:

"Yes. That's true. I'm about to be engaged to a girl in London called Cherry Mitchell. . . ."

CHAPTER TWELVE

By a happy chance the Vicar of Saint Saviour's had chosen as the text for his sermon *'The fruits of the earth and the fulness thereof'*, and Mr. Mitchell, sitting piously in the seventh pew from the front, wholly approved of his sentiments. In spite of the suitability of the sermon, he was conscious every now and again of a twinge of conscience. Had he done right in locking Cherry up? After all, she wasn't a little girl any more. She'd be twenty-three Friday. Should he not have talked to her gently, the way the late Mrs. Mitchell would have done? Young people had become more independent nowadays, and it was up to the older ones to make allowances. As well as that, Jim would be home tonight, and Jim was just what she needed, a decent, steady man who'd look after her. Normally of a Sunday morning he paid a brief and dignified visit to The Hand and Flower for a glass of sherry after church. Before the sermon was over, he had decided to forgo this pleasant habit for once. He'd go straight home and unlock Cherry's door and pat her on the shoulder and let bygones be bygones, and then they'd go off together to Aunty Flo's. After all, what was it the Vicar had said? *'Let not the sun go down on thy wrath.'* It was a good Christian exhortation, and one which he would surely follow. He joined in the singing of the final hymn with more than his usual fervour, and hurried home without even stopping to congratulate the Vicar on his morning address.

Mr. Mitchell entered the house by the hall door. At the foot of the stairs, a kindly thought struck him and he turned back and went into the shop. No good doing things by halves. He had remembered that Cherry was always partial to a nice peach, and he picked a specially succulent one from the box he reserved for his special customers. Bearing this olive branch in his hand, he walked upstairs on tiptoe and tapped on Cherry's door.

There was no sound from her room.

Ah well, sulky. . . .

He tapped again and said, "Cherry."

Silence. Maybe she was asleep. Poor kid. And she'd had no breakfast. He knocked a little louder.

"May I come in, dear? It's Dad, and I've got a nice peach for you."

There was no sound. Mr. Mitchell began to feel extraordinarily foolish. A ghastly thought slid suddenly into his mind and an icy hand seemed to settle over his heart. She . . . she couldn't have committed suicide. She couldn't. Not Cherry. He hammered on her door and shouted:

"I'm opening your door and I'm coming in. Do you hear me?"

In the quiet of Sunday he could hear the buses changing gear up in the Finchley Road. With shaking fingers he groped for the key in his pocket, found it, turned it in the lock and flung the door open.

The room was empty.

He stumbled across to the open window and looked out, fearful of what he expected to see. The yard, thank God, was as empty as her room. He sat down on the bed and drew a long, shuddering breath. Some minutes had passed before he noticed a folded sheet of paper stuck into the corner of the looking-glass. It was a receipt from C & A Modes and it was addressed to 'Dad'. With knees that had turned to water, he crossed the room once again, and took the note and opened it.

Dear Dad, I am going out with the boy I have a date with. Not that I like him because I don't. But it's not right for you to lock me in, it's not right. The chop for your dinner is in the frig. From your loving daughter Cherry.

P.S. The fathers have eaten a sour grape and the children's teeth are set on edge. Jeremiah 31, *verse* 29.

Corporal Marvin P. Lewes, United States Air Force, looked with ever-increasing admiration at Cherry Mitchell as she picked delicately at her Russian salad and told him the story of her Sunday morning. Looking at her blinking prettiness and listening to her voice, Marvin had to keep on reminding himself with incredulity that this English girl had literally dropped into his arms. The extraordinary circumstances of their meeting appealed irresistibly to his innate sense of the romantic. Only three things were wrong. It should have been a castle wall rather than a drain-pipe, his Jeep should have been a horse and Cherry herself should have been a refugee from Stalin.

Marvin was tall, lean-faced and courteous.

A direct descendant of one of the intrepid pilgrims who put out from Bristol for Plymouth Rock, he called cousin with the family in Somerset whose name he bore. He was a typical New Englander as far as any one individual can represent a group of nine and a half million persons, ranging from the lobster fishermen of Maine to the Brahmins of Boston. Despite vast divergence in breeding, speech and occupation, certain well-defined characteristics not only remained constant but even hardened over the centuries, and Marvin was heir to them all. He believed in work, thrift, honesty and physical endurance. He had three fierce, indivisible loyalties, which came in this order—Maine, New England, the United States—and if indeed the Pilgrim Fathers first fell on their knees and then on the aborigines, they did it because of an entrenched and very proper sense of duty. He was a studious, serious man with a taste for guide-books and parish registers, and this was the first time he had ever entertained any Englishwoman even remotely approximating to Cherry's age and appearance. He found the experience exhilarating. He had taken tea with antiquarian spinsters in Stratford-on-Avon and consumed nut cutlets with the widow of the incumbent of Coombedown. He had been shown the Oxford colleges by a don's sister, and the Cambridge colleges by an elderly archæologist in sandals and a fringed shawl. Cherry was something quite new, and her story summoned up all that shy chivalry of which he was secretly a little ashamed. To Cherry's cinematically tutored eye, he looked a little like a younger Gary Cooper. This resemblance did not stop at his personal appearance for, by an odd coincidence, he seemed to have a number of Mr. Cooper's more engaging mannerisms.

When her voice stopped, he said with the last remnants of suspicion fading.

"And you're quite sure your Pop isn't a Communist?"

"Quite sure. Actually Dad always votes for Mr. Churchill. But it wasn't right of him to lock me in. I'll be twenty-three Friday."

"I'll say it wasn't right! Do you know what it says in the American Declaration of Independence?"

"No. At least, not exactly."

"Well, listen to this." He cleared his throat and began with great solemnity, "It says, '*that all men are endowed by their*

Creator with certain unalienable Rights, that amongst these are Life, Liberty and the Pursuit of Happiness'. Those, Cherry, are the words of Thomas Jefferson, spoken on the 4th day of July, 1776."

"How did he know?" said Cherry with interest.

"How did who know what?"

"How did Mr. . . . Mr. Jefferson know what God had endowed people with? Dad says that this world is meant to be a vale of tears."

"Then, with great respect, Cherry, your Pop can't have been to the United States, nor can he know the American Way-of-Life."

"No, that's true. Dad's never been abroad." It occurred to Cherry that there might be an implied criticism of England in what Marvin had said, and she rose at once to the defence of her country. "As a matter of fact," she said tartly, "we have a thing like that too, but we don't blame God for it. It's called 'Magna Carta', and I learned about it at school."

"Magna Carta is a most noble document." Marvin felt in his pocket and took out a little blue reference book and spun the pages expertly. "That Magna Carta is a noble document, I would be the last to deny." He read aloud in a deep, sonorous voice:

"'*John, by the grace of God, King of England, Lord of Ireland, Duke of Normandy and Aquitaine, and Count of Anjou . . . to His Faithful Subjects, greetings. . . . We have also granted to all the freemen of our kingdom, for us and our heirs for ever, all the unwritten liberties, to have and to hold, them and their heirs, of us and our heirs. . . .*'

That was written on the 15th day of June, 1215."

"It's very pretty," said Cherry. "Like poetry. What does it mean?"

"Same thing as our Declaration of Independence."

"But ours came first," said Cherry. "I mean, it did, didn't it?"

"Yes, Miss Cherry. Yours came first." This was a girl of spirit, and he admired her for it. He admired her more and more with every passing minute. He offered her a cigarette from a paper packet, flipping the bottom of the packet so that the cigarette jumped out. His fingers were slim and dexterous as he lit her cigarette and then his own. He leaned forward.

"Tell me one thing," he said. "Before your Pop locked you up, why didn't you go to your Mom?"

"I haven't got a . . . a . . . Mom. She died years ago. And I call what you call my 'Pop' my 'Dad'."

"No Mom!" Marvin shook his head slowly. "Poor kid. That certainly is tough."

It was with a reinforced gush of sympathy that Marvin considered Cherry. To be the victim of a brutal father was bad enough, but to be without a Mom was the ultimate cruelty. To be deprived of a silver-haired lady in a rocking-chair, with an accommodating shoulder and an all-embracing philosophy, was too much. His generous heart warmed to this courageous orphan. And she was pretty, pretty as a picture. She certainly was. He became aware that the band was playing 'The Blue Danube' and realised for the first time that 'The Blue Danube' was his favourite waltz. Outside the sun shone on London, and to him, Marvin P. Lewes, had been vouchsafed the honour of saving this beautiful girl who might easily have fallen and broken her neck if he hadn't been there—in the nick of time. His mood of sympathy was replaced by one of masculine protectiveness and that, in its turn, by one of stern decision. He said in incisive tones:

"You say you've got a date this afternoon."

Cherry blinked. This was a new Marvin P. Lewes, and a much more pleasing one than the man with swimmy eyes. Much. She said in a small voice:

"Well yes. I suppose I have. In a way."

"With the guy with the motor-bike."

"Yes."

"Ditch him," said Marvin curtly. "He's just a wolf."

When Marvin got moving, he certainly went places. And he was quite right, too. Stan *was* a wolf. Funny she'd never realised it before. She'd always had a hidden hankering after masterful men—if they were kind as well—and Marvin was kind. She said meekly:

"Very well, Marvin. Just as you say."

"Right. That's that. Now tell me about the other guy, the one who left you alone and went off to France."

"Jim. Well, his name's Jim Carver and he's the steady sort. He's not a wolf like Stan. I don't think Jim's the sort who ever goes for young ladies much. It isn't only me. I don't think he goes for any young ladies. He's only really interested in the country really—the country and cows."

"Drink up your coffee," said Marvin, "and we'll get out of this dump into God's fresh air."

"Very well, Marvin."

The only three cities in the United States that Cherry had heard much about were New York, Chicago and Hollywood, and she had acquired her less than elementary knowledge of these from the screen. New York had the Statue of Liberty and skyscrapers, Chicago had gangsters and slaughter-houses and Hollywood had film stars. The only live Americans she had ever had the chance to ignore frigidly were the playful G.I.s who frequent Piccadilly Circus. Americans, therefore, were either District Attorneys (who were good) or tough guys (who were bad) or cowboys (who were mainly good—specially if they were sheriffs). All had a deep respect for their mothers. It was a frightening and stimulating thought to Cherry that Marvin fitted into only the last of these categories.

She had always had a contempt for those of her Anglo-Saxon sisters who hung around on the arms of Top-Sergeants whose stripes were upside down, anyway. An English girl should keep herself to herself, and if she didn't want to do that, what was wrong with an English boy from the 8th Army, anyway? You knew where you were with an English boy. The bewildering thought came to her that she knew equally well where she was with Marvin.

She sat beside him on the scorched grass of Regent's Park, and listened while he talked to her about the State of Maine with an enthusiasm that would have been naïve were it not so transparently sincere. He had a wealth of statistics at his finger-tips, and he produced one numerical fact after another. The State of Maine was practically as big as all the other five States in New England put together. It covered an area of sixty-six thousand six hundred and eight square miles, of which seventeen million acres were forest, roamed by more than one hundred and fifty thousand deer. The number of lakes was over two thousand five hundred, and the number of fish in these lakes ran into billions. New England was also the seat of the two greatest universities in the world, Harvard and Yale and . . .

"What about Oxford and Cambridge?" said Cherry,

dreamily. "I'm Cambridge, by the way. In the boat-race, I mean."

"Neither Oxford nor Cambridge—both of them excellent institutions," said Marvin magnanimously, "can compare with Harvard or Yale. Harvard has over eleven thousand students and Yale over eight thousand."

"Still, Cambridge did beat them in the boat-race last year, and in America itself," said Cherry. "I mean, Cambridge did, didn't it?"

"We too have a Cambridge, in New England, in the State of Massachusetts."

"Maybe," said Cherry obstinately, "but I bet it's not up to our Cambridge all the same."

For some little time Cherry had heard an intermittent snarling and roaring from within the confines of the nearby Zoo. As the minutes passed, the noise became constant, filling the air with menace. The lions' feeding-time was nigh, and she, who'd always been taken to the Zoo for her birthday treat, could almost see the tawny, excited beasts padding up and down their cages, slavering and twitching, waiting for the trolley-load of red meat to roll up to the clanging bars. And the way they fell on the meat once they got it, digging their claws in and sort of cuddling it and licking the blood. She gave a little shiver. Marvin said solicitously:

"Cold, honey?"

"No. Not cold. Aren't the lions awful?"

"Ah, the lions. It is on record that in the Bronx Park Zoo, New York, we have the finest lions in captivity in the world."

Cherry's feminine tremors were consumed by patriotism. She said with a certain acidity:

"I suppose you've got the fiercest tigers too and the most poisonous snakes and the biggest elephants?"

"That is so."

"Well, I don't believe it, not unless you put your elephants and our elephants on a scale and weighed them. Even then, ours would be the biggest. After all, I should know. I've ridden on one of ours—when I was a little girl, I mean."

"You certainly must have been cute when you were little," said Marvin warmly.

"Oh, I dunno. Not specially."

Now the roaring of the lions had risen to its crescendo, and Cherry was unable to divert a nervous glance from the direction of the Zoo. Marvin intercepted it. When she saw its effect on him, she didn't try. It rearoused all his protective instincts, and with the most altruistic of motives he put his strong arm around her shoulders and patted her gently. In no way did Cherry appear to resent this kindly attention, and by the time the roaring of the lions had subsided there seemed little reason for removing an arm into which Cherry's slim figure fitted so very snugly. Cherry tore a blade of grass into thin strips and plaited them with infinite care. She said casually:

"Tell me, Marvin, does your wife come from this Maine place, too?"

"My wife!" Marvin laughed. "Back home they used to rib me and say I was Chuppyville, Maine's most eligible bachelor. Well, honey, if that's true, I still am. Chuppyville's my home town. We've got a population of seventy-six thousand eight hundred and sixteen—I'm giving you figures correct to the 31st of December—and industry is centred round the Chuppyville Pulp and Paper Corporation, an undertaking of national importance, employing five thousand three——"

"Well, if you haven't got a wife," said Cherry idly, "what about your fiancée? Is she from Maine?"

"My fiancée." Marvin didn't laugh this time. His lean face became stern and his arm tightened a little around Cherry's pliant shoulders. "You want to know about my fiancée. O.K. Here we go. When I was drafted to England, I *was* engaged to a girl called Katey. We'd been in High School together, and our two families known each other all time, I guess. She weighed just a hundred and ten pounds and was as cute as cute. Well, I'd been in England just about two months—I'm on a ninety-day Duty Tour, by the way—when she sorta stopped writing. Then Wednesday three weeks back she did mail me—from Niagara Falls."

"But that's in Canada," said Cherry. "We had it in geography at school."

"Only some of it's in Canada. The other part—the better and bigger part—is in the United States, and you know what Niagara Falls is famous for?"

"Water?"

He shook his head.

"No. Not water. Honeymoons."

"But there's water there as well. I mean, isn't there?"

"Yes. It is estimated that every sixty seconds the rate of flow——"

"Never mind that," said Cherry practically. "Tell me about the honeymoon end of it."

"I have no practical experience of the honeymoon aspect of Niagara Falls," said Marvin bitterly. "But my fiancée Katey certainly has. She was there with a guy she'd married the night before in Buffalo, New York, a small-time drummer in caskets."

What was a 'drummer' and what were 'caskets'? It didn't matter. The big point was that the fickle Katey was now Mrs. Someone-or-other and that she was Miss Cherry Mitchell—with a thirty-four bust, twenty-four waist and thirty-six hips. Jim Carver shouldn't go off to France like that for the day and leave her, not if he was a real he-man he shouldn't. Her slender shoulders stiffened, and it occurred to Marvin that this English girl must weigh just about a hundred and ten pounds or maybe even a bit less. But whatever she tipped the scale at, it was distributed in the right places. It certainly was.

"Do you mean to say," said Cherry with righteous indignation, "that this Katey thing went off and carried on with another boy—and you abroad?"

"That's just what I do say." The descendant of a New England Puritan took over temporarily from a Corporal in the United States Air Force and Marvin spoke through the mouth of his ancestors. "*'Trust ye not in a friend, put ye not confidence in a guide: keep the doors of thy mouth from her that lieth in thy bosom.'*"

"Where?" said Cherry.

"*'In thy bosom',*" said Marvin with disapproval.

Cherry took a quick squint at her thirty-four-inch bust. She said in a small voice:

"Oh, I see."

A United States Air Force Corporal intercepted her downward glance, leapt the centuries and re-established his contemporary position.

"So do I. Right now."

Cherry said conversationally:

"You and my Dad should get together, Marvin. You and he would get on like a house on fire."

"I would be highly honoured to meet your Pop," said Marvin, "highly honoured, but I sail for home Wednesday. Why are you so confident that we'd hit it off?"

"Because you're both interested in the same things," said Cherry with a sniff. "If you see what I mean. Scripture about bosoms . . . about that sort of thing. I'm sorry you're leaving so soon, Marvin."

"I'm starting not to feel so good about it myself."

The *carnivora* of Regent's Park, glutted with horse-flesh, slept uneasily. The gibbons, swooping and whooping and leaping, took up the jungle call. Cherry relaxed. This was the country, the country as she liked it. She was sitting on the grass—and what could be more country than grass?—and the sky was above her with a bird singing, a skylark or a sparrow or something. There were plenty of animals, too, but they were in their proper place, in cages, where animals ought to be. Not walking about with horns, free to attack people. And when you got tired of being in the country, you could always get a 74 bus to Camden Town, or you could even take a taxi. Town and country—in Regent's Park you got the best of both. She said in a voice in which there was only the ghost of a hint of speculation:

"What's the name of the place you come from?"

Marvin's chest swelled. "Chuppyville, Maine."

"And is Chuppyville a town? I mean, it isn't in the country, is it?"

"Chuppyville, honey, has a population of——"

"I remember," she said quickly. "That means that it's a town."

"It's more than a town. It's the centre of a thriving industrial community, centred around the Chuppyville Pulp and Paper Corporation. Now envious citizens of other States may say—and do say!—that Chuppyville lacks culture. I'd like to tell you right now about the culture we've got in Chuppyville. We got the Chuppyville Glee Club, we got the Chuppyville Chaucer Circle, we got the Chuppyville Ladies' Metaphysical Centre——"

"Ladies' Centre," said Cherry with interest. "What do they talk about? Their tummy-buttons?"

Marvin looked at a decadent European with all the generous pity of one whose ancestors had escaped from a doomed continent. At the same time, he realised that anyone who said things like that would be either a riot in Chuppyville—or an all-time flop. And she'd said it innocently, just naturally, not to make a pass. Now Katey wouldn't have said a thing like that in a thousand years, and if she had, it would have been a pass, drawing attention to the way she was made. But not this English girl. She'd just said it. She'd said it simply. Marvin realised with blinding clarity that he was in the presence of someone who possessed an elemental innocence. The knowledge had an instantaneous and most disturbing effect on him. It set a match to that unsuspected stream of pure lunacy that ran like unlit petrol beneath the encrustations of a New England upbringing. In the light of the conflagration, he saw Cherry as a visionary might see Jeanne d'Arc—and he saw himself as the man destined to pluck her from the burning. He was going home on Wednesday—home to a Chuppyville from which Katey had fled. Gosh, suppose he didn't go alone. . . .

"This guy who went to France—you engaged to him?"

"No, Marvin. We just said we'd talk about it when he comes home tonight."

"Give him the air," said Marvin firmly. "And I guess I'd like to meet your Pop. But before I meet your Pop, I'd like to tell you right now about my Mom."

Cherry blinked. She knew enough about Americans to know that the conversation had suddenly taken a fantastic turn. Moms and marriage bells were synonymous.

"I'd like very much to hear about your mother," she said shyly.

"Well, let's get comfortable."

"I'm . . . I'm quite comfortable already."

"We could be more comfortable."

"Yes . . . I suppose so. Oh, Marvin. . . ."

The gibbons, their play over, were silent. The only sound was the singing of a skylark or a sparrow or something, a tiny fluttering speck in the summer sky, singing away like mad. Jim had no right to go away like that and leave her alone. Asking for trouble, that's what it was . . . and she'd be twenty-three Friday.

CHAPTER THIRTEEN

Marie-Josephe ran quickly up the stairs and along the passage to her grandmother's room. The grandmother was sitting in her high-backed chair by the window, her hands lightly clasped in her lap. There was about her a calmness, a sort of timeless serenity, that was wholly at variance with Marie-Josephe's eager mood, and it was with difficulty that she checked the impatience that quickened her words.

"You wish to speak to me, Grandmère?"

"Yes, Marie-Josephe." She indicated a chair with an unhurried, deliberate gesture of her hand, reclasped her fingers in her lap. "Sit down, child."

Marie-Josephe tried not to glance at the clock on the mantelpiece. It was a clock she had always loved and one that would one day be hers, but now she bitterly resented every delicate movement of its mechanism as it snipped the precious seconds away, as if with sharp scissors. She tried to look anywhere in the room other than towards the mantelpiece—and failed. The hands of the clock pointed to three. Jim's boat sailed for England, for the other end of the world, at a quarter-past six. All that was left to them was a bare three and a quarter hours, a hundred and ninety-five fugitive minutes. Madame Berthier intercepted her granddaughter's glance. She said gently and with great affection, speaking in English:

"Even if I were to stop the hands of the clock for you, Marie-Josephe, it would do nothing to arrest the passage of time."

Marie-Josephe frowned in bewilderment. Again that extraordinary fluency, again that hint of an Irish brogue.

"Forgive me, Grandmère. It was not polite of me. Please forgive me."

"There is nothing to forgive. It is a glance I would have given had I been you at this time. More than that, it is a glance I have many times given when I was younger than I am today." The dark eyes glimmered. "But believe me, Child, it is better for Henri, better for the Englishman, Jim, that you stay here, even for a few minutes."

Marie-Josephe looked sharply at her grandmother.

These were strange words to hear from the puckered lips of an old lady, and Marie-Josephe saw her lined face with a new perception.

She had always been there, as unchanging as the straight-backed chair in which she invariably sat by the window. She had always been old, old as her chair or her clock were old, immortal as the youth of a child was immortal. She was 'Grand-mère'—and Grandmère was not a person. Grandmère was a terrible teacher of manners, a timely provider of gingerbread and nougat, a mender of torn frocks, a figure on whose dry breast one could surprisingly cry away a toothache. Now, all of a minute, she had changed. Youth had come upon her, and Marie-Josephe saw her own face reflected. She seemed to see the wrinkles dissolve into smooth skin, she saw the nascent fire in the dark eyes, she realised with a sense almost of shock that the dry breast had once been divided and springing and young. It was a glimpse that startled her, and humbled her and drew her strongly to the woman in the straight-backed chair. She said freely, speaking without restraint to one from whom no secret was hidden.

"But we have so little time."

"That you don't know. Who can say? It is possible that you have a lifetime before you."

Marie-Josephe was silent. After a moment she said in a curiously still voice:

"I cannot believe you. I do not deserve such a thing."

Her grandmother said with a sigh:

"If it had been the purpose of God to see that all men and women got what they deserved, why did He send His Son? Do you think, child, that Henri Dubot deserves you? Do you think that he deserves a young girl to be his bride?"

"I do not wish to think of this thing. I cannot believe that it will be true."

"That I do not know." She paused. "I do know that I have done you a great wrong."

"It is impossible that you could do me a wrong."

"It is true. When Henri wished to marry you, he approached your father. Because I am who I am, your father—my son—came to me to seek my counsel. It is, as you know, how these matters are usually arranged. Your father and I talked long over this question. At first, he was doubtful of giving you, a young and inexperienced girl, to the hands of a man who has, let us say, lived fully. Your father wished you to be found by a man who would love you and whom you would love with . . . with magic. But in France, *Grandmère de la famille* has great power, and I persuaded him otherwise. I spoke, child, from my brain and not from my heart. I had forgotten many things. I saw for you a position, children, material security, servants, the envy of others. I must frankly tell you, Child, that I saw other things, too. I thought it unlikely that you would permanently retain the fidelity of a sophisticated man. But you, as a recompense, you would have your home and your children and, the world being what it is, you would have a certain measure of happiness. I balanced all—with my brain."

Madame Berthier paused. She looked out of the window into the sunshine. When she turned round, her voice was full of pain:

"I was a wicked woman, Marie-Josephe, because I was committing a sin against the light."

Let the clock tick the precious minutes away. If there were to be a lifetime before them, Marie-Josephe would gladly give these few moments to someone she loved. And if the space with Jim were to be brief, how could one grudge of its brevity to one from whose eyes tears were not far distant?

"I am an old woman, sitting in a chair by the window. But I was not always like that. Marie-Josephe, give me your hand. I talk in English to you today, for that is the language to which what I say belongs. It is a great joy for me to speak English.

"I married your grandfather when I was twenty. It was an arranged marriage and one without enchantment. My son, your father, was born a year later. It is the practice of the Germans to despoil France from time to time, and in 1914 the Boches came to visit us. My husband was called to the Thirty-third Regiment of Infantry. He was killed on the 23rd October, in the battle of Artois. My age then was twenty-seven years. I had long ago sent my son to a safe place. I was still young, a widow and alone, and it was in a hospital behind Arras that I met my friend. We grew to love each other deeply. He was a British officer, an Irishman in the regiment of the West, the Connaught Rangers, and he had been wounded. When he could leave hospital, he came to me. It was a small, very quiet place, far from the war, with many birds in the gardens and a stream of trout. He tried each day, but never did he catch a single trout. We had many weeks together, each day of great and increasing happiness. He wished very much to marry me and take me and my son to his home in Ireland."

Madame Berthier was sitting bolt upright in her chair. She said proudly in the English of another day:

"He was a most honourable gentleman and my dear friend."

Marie-Josephe's hand tightened a little around the dry fingers. The clock and the ticking of the clock were no longer of any importance, for there might be an infinity of years before her.

"He wished me to be his wife and my son to be his son. I believed, in my foolishness, yes and in my cruelty, that it was too much to ask that a man should take on the child of another man. I believed that a man, in his heart, would come to resent the child that was not of his own creation. I did not realise that, in ultimate truth, I, a mother, had come to him as a young girl and that he was my first and only love. So I sent him away."

"And he went."

"Yes, he went. Though his wounds had been so deep that he was released from service for ever, he returned to England and he persuaded the British Army that he was still able to fight. It was not difficult. It was in the black spring before victory, and men, even ill men, were welcomed for the battle. He came back to France. We never met again. He was killed, oh, very quickly. He sleeps among the men of his regiment, the Connaught Rangers, close to where you found your friend Jim, close to where your brother lies, in the *Cimetière de l'Est.*" She paused. "It is as if the Germans, Kaiser and Hitler, had chosen this hillside over Boulogne as a *rendezvous* for our family and for those we love."

The chickens still pecked under the farm-cart in the heat of the summer afternoon. It seemed that the shadow of the shafts had moved not at all. A bare ten minutes had served to encompass so many years of hollowness and grief. Marie-Josephe stood up. She said gently:

"Now give me your counsel, Grandmère."

"Do nothing that you would not wish to do for ever."

"I think I understand what you wish to say to me." Her heart was light and she said, laughing, "It was you, Grandmère, who taught me to sing *'Savez-vous planter les choux'*."

"Yes, child, that is true. But what of it?"

"It is a pretty song. I like it very much. And now you permit me to leave you?"

"Of course."

Marie-Josephe kissed her grandmother's forehead, not formally but with love. She said:

"Au revoir, Grandmère. Et merci."

CHAPTER FOURTEEN

It was some little time before Jim Carver realised that the barometer on the wall of the dining-room must be broken. Despite the fairness of the day, the needle pointed steadily to '*Tempête*', and that seemed to him to be a reasonably accurate description of the situation rapidly developing between him and Henri Dubot.

Mademoiselle Mitchell was the first subject for enquiry. She was blonde or brunette?

"Blonde."

"Ah." Henri who was, as the sergeant saw, the willing captive of a brunette, confessed that he too found blondes delicious. Mademoiselle Mitchell's hair was possibly the colour of champagne?

"Well . . . possibly."

"Mademoiselle is tall, short?"

"Well, neither. Something between the two."

In an attempt to clarify the next question, Henri undulated his hands over the front of his black jacket and said:

"She 'as a figure like this, yes?"

Jim Carver put down his glass with a slight clatter. He had no wish to discuss Cherry at all. That a stranger should speak of her in these terms was quite intolerable. He said slowly and very distinctly:

"In England, Monsieur Dubot, it is not the custom to refer to one's friends in this way, and I would be grateful if we might change the subject."

Henri was visibly discomposed. His hands fluttered in apology.

"I excuse myself infinitely. We will speak instead of one 'oo we both know. We will speak of Marie-Josephe. I propose to marry myself with her in the month of October. We will go for our 'oneymoon to the *Côte d'Azur*, to Cannes, in my car. You 'ave been to Cannes?"

"No. Never."

"It is very beautiful. In France, one calls Cannes 'the city, the town of flowers and of elegant sports'. I 'ave already reserve our *appartement*. It is one with a balcony. From the balcony, at night, one can listen to the music from the terrace below while one regards the moon and the stars. There also, on this balcony, each morning we will take our *petit déjeuner,* our small breakfast, and regard the sea."

"I hope," said Jim Carver huskily, "that it keeps fine for you."

For a moment Henri did not understand. Then his face cleared and he laughed.

"You 'ope that it keeps fine. As for me, I 'ope not! If it is beautiful, Marie-Josephe and I will no doubt promenade ourselves on the *Croisette,* but if it is unbeautiful, we will rest in our *appartement,* with many flowers. Figure to yourself. Mimosa, roses—and Marie-Josephe. I 'ope for rain! But I speak too much of ourselves, of Marie-Josephe and me. How of you and Mademoiselle Mitchell? You will go where for your 'oneymoon? I do not know the cities of England. You will go to Birmingham? To Blackpoule?"

Jim lit a cigarette. There was a long pause. When he spoke, his voice was steady:

"Some minutes ago, I suggested a change of conversation. I said that one didn't discuss women one was fond of in so . . . so personal a way. Do you not think we could find some other subject?"

"But my dear Sergeant——"

"And one more thing. I am not a sergeant. The war is over and my name is Jim Carver."

"I regret infinitely." He shrugged in mock helplessness. "We may not speak of Mademoiselle Mitchell and we may not speak of Marie-Josephe. Of the war we may not speak because you wish no longer to be a sergeant." He lifted a forefinger. "Ah! I 'ave a good idea. We will speak of this game, this game that you play in The Hand and Flower, this game of darts. I am myself very sportif. Please explain to me this game."

"You want to know about darts." Jim frowned. He wished to God that Marie-Josephe would come back. He launched into a description of darts, increasingly aware of the inadequacy of his words. Darts was a game played indoors, in English pubs. There was a round board with numbers on the circumference, from one to twenty. You threw your darts, things like arrows, three—one after the other—at the board, trying to get the high numbers. Then you added up what you'd scored and subtracted the sum from three hundred and one, starting and going out on a double.

Henri passed his fingers through his hair. He looked like a student of modern languages who had had the calculus laboriously explained to him in Byzantine Greek. He said, shaking his head:

"And you play this . . . this darts very often?"

"Oh yes. People play it quite a bit. It's really quite simple."

"Evidemment!" He clearly hadn't understood a word. "And you come all the way from London to Boulogne to play this game?"

"Not exactly. The club came more or less for a holiday."

Henri Dubot smiled. "After so much mathematics, your Club will 'ave need of a 'oliday. Now you, Mr. Carver, you 'ad the good chance to meet Marie-Josephe. But your friends, 'ow will they occupy themselves in Boulogne? Boulogne is not very gay, and I ask myself, what will your friends do?"

What would they do? To his surprise, Jim realised that he hadn't the faintest idea. Only four were immutable: Mr. Hetherington, Mr. Thomson, Mr. Johnson and Mr. Pratt would go on playing bridge. If they were allowed to stay on board, they wouldn't even come ashore. But wherever they were, the cards would be spread. Once lunch was over, what would the others do? How would Charley Brewer dispose of his few hours in a French port, what would the genial Trevor Hilgrove do, Luke Grenfell and his enemy Shorty, Mr. Collins himself? He, Jim Carver, had had a definite purpose in coming to this town. But what about the others? He said slowly, his brow in a tangle:

"Now that you ask me, I don't really know. I expect they'll all stick together and just look at the shops. . . ."

After his altercation with the owner of the corset shop, Charley Brewer had come to the conclusion that the French couldn't take a joke. He'd only given a tug at the suspenders for a lark. No need to come the acid and create. Never mind. Here he was in a French market-place, he'd still got his dough and his mouth-organ, and surely among the teeming crowds he'd find someone prepared to succumb to one or the other of these lures. He wiped the sweat off his forehead, replaced his bowler hat with a devil-may-care tilt and boldly entered the market.

He was cast down by what he saw.

Back home in England, you thought of France as being entirely populated by the sort of young ladies you saw in penny-in-the-slot machines on piers, but once you actually got here and had a look around, you might as well be at a church social or something. They all looked so blooming motherly. Of course, it was different at night. Everyone knew that. At night, the whole of France was covered with a rash of red lamps like a kid with the measles. Fat lot of good that was when the boat sailed at a quarter-past six.

He stopped morosely by a bric-à-brac stall presided over by a sunburned, deep-bosomed Amazon of about thirty. Her stock consisted of nude celluloid dolls jumbled up with emblems of piety. The dolls—all of which were undeniably lady dolls—had what seemed to be human hair, and all wore tiny sun-glasses. His attention soon wandered from these inanimate objects to their vendor. Without committing himself to speech, Charley decided to indicate his wish to know her better. With his bowler hat on the back of his head and his rose drooping, he began to indicate by smirks, winks and by white gym-shoe shuffling, that her appearance was not displeasing to him. The Amazon stood it for as long as she could. As soon as she noticed that her colleagues in the market had also remarked on the fact that this—this hippopotamus had constituted himself as her admirer, she decided to bring the matter to an end. She looked around the market and called shrilly:

"Ou est mon mari? Gabriel, viens ici."

A giant of a man in a blue jersey put down the knife with which he had been gutting mackerel, wiped his bloody hands on his apron and shambled over to the stall. Charley's heart sank into his gym shoes. The word 'mari' had an unmistakable echo of church organs and orange blossom, and it occurred to him that the quicker he was away from here the better. Husband and wife had hardly exchanged a word before Charley's bowler hat was once again tucked underneath his arm and his gym shoes were glimmering down the rue Something-or-other in the opposite direction from the bric-à-brac stall and the gut-boards of the market.

Trevor Hilgrove sat in the *Café Gérard* pretending to read the *News of the World*, waiting for Pierre Jumelle to indicate which of the familiar four methods of transferring his illegal merchandise he wished to employ. The ball was at Pierre's feet. It was up to him to kick it.

Trevor took a deep swig of his beer, folded up the *News of the World* and put it on the table and yawned. He looked lazily round the café. Almost immediately, Pierre appeared to lose interest in *Combat* and put the paper in his pocket. He glanced at Trevor and stretched out his hand towards the discarded *News of the World*. He said politely:

"Vous permettez, Monsieur?"

Trevor started. He frowned as if he only half-understood.

"What is it, old chap? Want my paper?"

Pierre nodded. He began in slow, very careful French:

"S'il vous plait, Monsieur. I derive much pleasure in reading the English newspapers. I read them always three times."

Trevor understood instantly. He said politely:

"Do have the paper. I've finished it. Read it three times, like you do."

"Pardon, Monsieur?"

"I, too, have read it three times. *Comprenez?"*

"Si, si. Je comprehends. Parfaitement."

Pierre took up the *News of the World* and opened it with great care. Lying coyly beside the account of a Scoutmaster's eccentricities was the slim wad of United States ten-dollar bills that he expected to see. By no flicker of the eyelid did he indicate that there was anything in the paper other than the parade of human frailty. He refolded it leisurely and took up his plump despatch-case. He said with a little bow.

"I may keep this journal?"

"Wee, wee, old boy. Keep it by all means."

"Merci, Monsieur. You are most kind. *Au revoir."*

"Oh revoor," said Trevor cordially.

The first part of 'Operation Timepiece' had gone with a swing. The second and most difficult part would start in about three minutes—for Pierre was a fast worker. He stood up and bowed again, and made his way between the tables to the swing door marked TOILETTES et TELEPHONE, entered. Trevor saw the door rock on its hinges as he vanished. He glanced at his watch. Say two and a half minutes. . . .

It was at that moment that General Felix de la Chanterelle was compelled to enter the *Café Gérard* for the first time in his life. Although the General bore malice towards no man, he was to be the innocent instrument whereby Trevor's most carefully designed schemes were to be confounded.

Shorty—who was drinking a clouded yellow liquid that tasted of aniseed—looked around him and at his companion with a recurring sense of amazement. He had never been out of England before in his life, and now, here he was, in France. Outside in the streets of Boulogne, the people were French people, talking the French language and thinking nothing of it. Even the kids spoke it, jabber, jabber, jabber, as to the manner born. The incredible fact that he was actually in France paled into insignificance compared with the even more extraordinary fact that he was sitting in a café in France with Mr. Luke Bloody Grenfell—and liking it. He put down his glass. With a touch of his old truculence he said:

"What's this muck called?"

"Pernod."

"Huh." He rapped loudly on the table at the waiter. "Two more of these. Toot sweet."

"One's enough for me, Shorty. Powerful stuff, Pernod."

"You'll take another—and like it," said Shorty in his tough voice. "Well bung-ho—or as my Dad used to say—'down the hatch'."

"Down the hatch."

Luke lit a *Gauloise.* Now that the long enmity between him and Shorty seemed to be dissolving, he could go back to the contemplation of France. Even at school he had begun to read the French poets with joy, if without profound comprehension, believing that knowledge of a foreign nation's literature gave some knowledge of that foreign nation's mind. The verse of the French Renaissance was not only startling in its clear recognition of the temper of its time, but derivative as well. It derived from something rooted in the French memory. It was as old as a bush and as fresh as a handful of spring water.

"Mr. Grenfell."

Luke sighed. He said, "Yes, Shorty."

"I happened to be passing by Burkley Square a week or two back and I saw you."

"Did you? Why didn't you say 'Hi'?"

"You'd a lady with you and you were driving a three-litre Bentley sports." He sniffed. "Nice job she was. Short chassis."

Luke chuckled. "The lady—or the Bentley?"

"Both."

"That was my young sister, Chloe. Nice child."

Shorty's jaw dropped.

"Your young sister!"

"Certainly. Why not? People have sisters, you know."

"But, for Gawd's sake, she called you 'darling'. I heard her with my own two ears."

"She wanted to borrow something, that's all. You always want to mind your eye when your baby sister calls you 'darling'."

"Blimey," said Shorty. "Some baby!"

He thought of his own sister—or rather half-sister—with an emotion akin to hatred. Beryl was a mealy-mouthed little slut who worked by day in a shop in the Edgware Road, and who came out at night to hang about the doors of West End restaurants and pester film stars for their autographs. There was nothing she wouldn't do to get the careless scribble, "Good luck, Beryl," from any one of these demi-gods, male or female. She would hang on to the door-handle of their cars, mouthing and fawning—and ring up those who refused to contribute to her neurosis from anonymous call-boxes in the middle of the night to dribble obscenities down the telephone. Shorty gave a brief, sardonic laugh.

"What's the joke, Shorty?"

"I was just thinking what *my* sister would say if I called her 'my angel'."

"What would she say?"

Shorty told him. There was a long silence between them. Then Luke said gently:

"That's not pretty, is it?"

"I didn't say it was, did I? There's a lot in London that's not pretty, but you wouldn't know about that."

"Wouldn't I?"

"No, you wouldn't."

Shorty stared out into the sunny street. He saw nothing of France. He saw himself imprisoned for ever in the only London he knew, plying the only trade he knew. He saw himself standing on the corners of mean streets or in the doorways of mean houses, waiting for the mugs to sidle up to him with their 'tanner each way Lovely Bubbles and anything to come, half-a-crack Golden Tangle, four-thirty', and having to keep an eye skinned all the time for a copper and being ready to run like hell. . . . There wasn't much future in England for anyone who worked for a gentleman like Mr. McIsaac, especially with the winter coming on. Up to now, Mr. McIsaac had paid the fines, but he wouldn't go on doing it, not for ever, he wouldn't, and then where would Shorty be?

A thought slid into his mind and stayed there quivering. It would be all right if he could stay here, here in France, where nobody knew him and he could make a fresh start. He was only twenty-four and tough. He flexed his biceps so that the knotted muscles became rigid. He'd say he was tough. But you couldn't stay here in France with no job and no dough. You were always caught, no matter where you were, if you'd no job and no dough. But, blimey, it would be all right if you could stay here, or go somewhere, anywhere, and make a fresh start. . . .

"Let's push on, Shorty."

"O.K."

They happened to pass by a bookshop and Luke stopped. While he was looking at an uncut edition of André Gide, Shorty idly picked up another book off the counter—and in doing so changed the whole course of his life, utterly and irrevocably.

Henri Dubot looked at Jim Carver quizzically, his head on one side.

"You consider that your friends will stay together and regard the windows of the shops. In Boulogne, we are much experienced with the arrival of the English, and it is not the shops they seek, these gentlemen on 'oliday. Oh no."

"Then what do they seek?" said Jim curtly.

"They seek, per'aps, what they do not find in England."

"Meaning what?"

"The same thing that a Frenchman on 'oliday in England might seek. They wish for a small, a discreet, romance. . . ."

Upstairs a door opened and shut. Quick footsteps, the hurrying footsteps of Marie-Josephe, sounded on the bare boards of the passage over their heads, and they heard her turn round the top of the banisters and come running downstairs. She jumped the last two steps and swung the dining-room door open. She said breathlessly:

"I am so sorry. I was a long time with Grandmère. But it

was very important that I should stay." She advanced into the room. "Henri, it is surely time for you to go. Jim, you have had some Benedictine and you have been having English conversation with Henri. That is excellent."

"What is this important matter with Grandmère?" said Henri sharply. "It concerns me?"

"Oh no, Henri. I . . . I don't think so. It was something which Grandmère wished to talk to me about. But you know you are late. You must go to your client at half-past three, and already it is more than a quarter-past. I shall feel that I am to blame if you are late."

"I will go and make my adieux immediately. Then I will drive you and . . . your friend, Sergeant Carver, to Boulogne to attend the vessel for England."

"But, Henri, do you not think it would be better for me to go in the Renault? Papa has told me to take some lettuce and a sack of potatoes to Madame Loget in the town, and I know that you do not permit our farm produce in your car."

He looked at her irresolutely and then at his watch. He said sharply:

"Please to await me, Marie-Josephe. I return in three minutes and then I wish to speak with you alone."

"But of course."

When he had gone, Marie-Josephe came to where Jim stood. Never in his life could he have imagined anyone more beautiful or more radiant. She held out her two hands and he took them in his. Without knowing it, she echoed her grandmother's words. She said simply:

"You are my dear friend, Jim."

"And you mine, Marie-Josephe."

CHAPTER FIFTEEN

MADAME BERTHIER continued to sit by the window of her room. Her hands, clasped in her lap, were motionless. Her black dress with its narrow white edging at the neck, her iron-grey hair and fine, wrinkled profile, could best have been represented by a steel engraving.

Many years had passed since she had permitted herself the painful joy of remembering, and now the long-dammed fountain of grief gushed and flowed freely in the deepest recesses of her mind. When she had heard casually, almost light-heartedly, from a Gunner Captain that her lover had fallen, she had not believed his words. It had been far beyond her comprehension to grasp that this man was mortal, or that his gay courtesy could ever be quenched. For weeks she had confidently awaited news of him and of the men he led. Regiments came and went, English regiments, Scottish, even Irish, but she never again heard the drums or the terrible cursing of the Connaught Rangers. The weeks of silence became months of silence and, after a long time, Madame Berthier began to die. She did it surely, without fuss and with great dignity.

When the Germans went home again, she saw her son, Louis. He was nearly ten years old, and to him and to his future she dedicated her brain and her muscles, all that was left of her to offer.

For what purpose did God give strength?

They had been hard, unremitting years, scarred by the obstinacy of the grudging fields. Plough, harrow, sow, reap, plough; roots, barley, oats, maize, roots; calf, heifer, cow, milk, calf. The rhythm of the seasons, each with its own back-breaking tasks, was as constant and as pitiless as were the weeds that sprang up to choke the young wheat. Miraculously, despite the untimely malice of snow and sun, of drought and of flood, order had begun to emerge out of disorder, profit out of loss. Her son, suddenly a man, had courted a simple, strong girl, and they had been married in the Church of Saint Xavier. Denis, *le petit* Denis, her grandson, had been born and then, after a space, Marie-Josephe. Now, surely, an ageing woman could begin to take to her high-backed chair.

But the itch that lay in the soles of the feet of the *Boches* was still uncured, and the march of the grey men, humourless as they were murderous, began once again. The work of years crumbled in a night, the night of the 12th of June, 1940. Madame Berthier's son, his fields pillaged and his fine cattle driven to a commandeered slaughter-house, limped to a forced labour camp in a Reich that was to last for a thousand years. The British had gone and the only washing hung on the Siegfried Line was the underclothing of women who had forgotten that they were Frenchwomen first and women afterwards. Her grandson Denis, *le petit* Denis, chose to take plastic rather than seed in his hands—and died in Lille under the new automatic Schmeisser of a Gestapo corporal.

A pretty weapon: *cin schönes Gewähr.*

When the British came again, Grandmère looked in vain for the Connaught Rangers. She could not know that a Regiment had died, as her lover had died. An old lady sitting at a window watching the tanks and the half-tracks and the three-tonners go by, could hardly be expected to realise that the sons of the Connaughtmen she had known were scattered over every Regiment and Corps in the British Army. How could she understand that the neutrals of Mayo and Galway and Clare leavened the Lancers and swore their terrible oaths from D-day to VE-day, and long after that? Timidly she had asked one of the young soldiers in the town where the Connaught Rangers were, the Connaught Rangers of the West of Ireland. The Cockney's answer had dumbfounded her. "Connaught Rangers? Never 'eard of 'em, lady." With characteristic good humour, he had reached out and grabbed a passing Irish Guardsman. " 'Ere, Mick, ever 'eard of a mob called the Connaught Rangers?" The Guardsman, a bullock of a man from Sligo, had said in a melancholy, sing-song voice, "Ach, thim's no more. But they were desperate fellers in their day and avid for fighting."

It was as good an epitaph as any.

Now, once more she heard steps on the bare boards of the passage. They were firm, decisive steps, the steps of a man whose feet were firmly on the ground. The knock on her door was sharp and authoritative. She did not turn her head or make any movement of her hands, but her lips spoke and tightened.

"*Entrez.*"

"I have come, Madame, to make my adieux."

"That is kind of you, Henri."

"Before I leave for Boulogne, there is something I wish to say."

"I am all attention."

"You, Madame, have considerable influence over Marie-Josephe, far more influence than her parents. You are . . . *Grandmère de la famille*. I now ask myself in what direction Grandmère chooses to exercise her influence."

"Please explain yourself, Henri."

"Marie-Josephe arrives home with this . . . . this friend, an Englishman, a sergeant, a person of no account. I am tolerant, and I accept him because he appears to be a friend of the family. One must, I suppose, be prepared to do these things. He is made welcome, more welcome than I have ever been made in this household. Let that pass. After lunch, Marie-Josephe finds it necessary to show him the farm and the animals of the farm. She makes him the friend of that savage beast, Siki, and Siki, like the rest of the family Berthier, lies down at the feet of the sergeant."

"It is to Siki that you should address your complaint, Henri. Is it your opinion that the dog should have bitten our guest?"

He looked at her sharply. Could it be that she was laughing at him? Her lined face was impassive and there was no hint of amusement in her dark eyes.

"No. I ask no such thing."

"I am relieved to hear it. Please continue."

"You wished to speak to Marie-Josephe and I send her to you—even though I am thereby forced into the society of this . . . this exalted visitor, this representative of the aristocratic English game of darts. You find it expedient, Madame, to keep your granddaughter with you for over a quarter of an hour. May one enquire the all-important subject of your conversation with my fiancée?"

She turned her head at last and looked at him solemnly.

"I think, Henri," she said gently, "that you forget to whom you speak."

"You refuse to tell me, Madame?"

She smiled.

"Of course. It is an impertinence that you should ask for the report of a conversation between my granddaughter and myself."

"Then I shall demand of Marie-Josephe that she tells me."

"You will 'demand'! In my eyes, Henri, you are becoming a very small person."

"Nevertheless, I will demand."

"You do not know, nor have you ever known, the quality of the person you wish to make your wife. Marie-Josephe will never break the confidence that I have reposed in her. I gave her not only a confidence but some advice. It was advice designed to rectify a wrong of which I am guilty, advice which, please God, will lead my granddaughter to great and lasting happiness."

"If Marie-Josephe refuses to tell me, I warn you, Madame, that I shall reconsider my position." He bowed. "*Au revoir, Madame.*"

"Good-bye, Henri," said Grandmère Berthier in English.

CHAPTER SIXTEEN

Henri Dubot came down the stairs and into the room. It was evident that he was labouring under considerable emotion, but exactly what that emotion was had yet to be revealed. He bowed with frigid politeness to Jim.

"You will forgive me, Monsieur, if I speak with my fiancée alone."

"Of course." Jim stood up. He was very much embarrassed. "Marie-Josephe, may I look at the farm and the cattle again?"

"Yes. Please do. But not at the boule. He has not yet got a . . . a spreader. Take Siki with you. I will come and find you."

"Very well."

He walked along the passage and out into the day. The sun, after the dimness of the house, was so bright that it seemed to pierce the pupils of his eyes, and he stood for a moment by the door, breathing deeply. Then he crossed the yard and took Siki off his chain. He walked, the dog at his heels, out of the gate and turned to the left along the road. He neither knew where he was going nor did he care. He came soon to the field of barley and stepped lightly along its grass verge for a few yards. By a rusted reaper-and-binder he sat down, leaning his back against its wheel, stretching out his legs. The sun beat fiercely on his face, and the very little wind that stirred the barley sometimes seemed to intensify the heat. Small sounds wove themselves into the afternoon, the thin singing of larks, the whirr of insects' wings, the panting of Siki by his side. He tangled his fingers in the dog's rough coat, and gazed over the levels of the barley towards the town and the uplifted, glimmering dome of *Notre Dame de Boulogne*.

With all his strength he wished to be with Marie-Josephe now, at this time. But he knew with bitterness that there was nothing he could do to sustain this girl who, a few hours ago, had been nothing but a name, a pinafore and the words of a song. To what smooth censure was she being subjected, this girl of grace, this proud person who, even in the presence of the man she would marry, moved always with an indefinable air of being alone? He said, speaking aloud into the afternoon:

"I want to be with her."

The sound of his voice seemed to break the spell of thought. The voice he had heard was the voice of Jim Carver, and Jim Carver had other things to think about than the unheard conversation between a French lawyer and his fiancée. He had Cherry Mitchell to think about, Cherry Mitchell in London, Cherry Mitchell waiting to hear the words which would bind him to her for ever. He knew now that those words would never be spoken.

He was not forsaking her for another person, because Marie-Josephe was as unattainable as a star. He would have to forsake her because, in the light of this miracle that had been revealed to him, it would be sinful for him to do anything else. To say the words of the marriage service out loud before God would be blasphemy. It would subject Cherry to the ultimate and lasting insult. He saw her already as he had seen his companions of The Hand and Flower, but through an even less transparent veil. Only Marie-Josephe was clear to him, only Marie-Josephe would remain clear to him in the loneliness and in the long muscular days of the future—and there could be no path other than a solitary one for the feet of an honest man.

Beneath his fingers, Siki's muscles moved. Jim looked round. He saw Marie-Josephe coming along the grass by the barley. She came beside him and sat down. She did not speak at all, but gazed over the burnished field. He became aware that she was trembling, and he could sense rather than see the quiver in her fingers. There was nothing he could do, absolutely nothing. He could only be—and try in stillness and silence to calm her with his strength and his devotion.

From the front of the farm they heard the sound of an engine starting up. Siki stiffened and growled in his throat. The noise of the engine snarled into a roar, changed into an angry hum. As a car turned into the road and took the hill on the road to Boulogne, Marie-Josephe became rigid. The dust of its going settled whitely on the corn, the sound bored into their eardrums harshly, receded, became a strident whine, died away, was replaced by the invisible needles of the larks singing.

Marie-Josephe stood up and faced Jim. She said in a voice

that was still uncertain of itself:

"We too must go to Boulogne. Will you please say good-bye to my parents and to my grandmother. Then we will go together. We have only a little more than two hours before you go away."

They walked side by side, remote from each other, along the road by which Henri's car had passed, entered the yard in that same silence. Jim put Siki on his chain, and patted his head in a sudden gush of affection. Monsieur and Madame Berthier were in the dining-room and cordial if slightly strained good-byes were said and a promise extracted that Jim would never again come to Boulogne without paying a visit to the farm, where he would always be most welcome.

"Now I will take you to the room of my grandmother. I consider it to be better that you should say good-bye to her by yourself. I will go to my room and do my hair, and meet you in a few minutes by the car."

"My French isn't terribly good, Marie-Josephe."

"You will not find that any problem." She tapped on the oak door and entered her grandmother's room. She said in English, "Jim wishes to say good-bye to you, Grandmère."

The old lady turned her head slowly.

"Please come over to me, to the window. I have your permission to call you 'Jim'?"

"Please do."

Marie-Josephe shut the door very quietly behind them and walked on tiptoe to her room. She sat down with a great sigh, and gazed at her face in the looking-glass. It seemed to her that she was looking at a stranger, a stranger from whose body all strength had been drained. Deliberately she refused to allow herself to think of what she had done. The implications were much too vast to be considered now while Jim's physical, breathing presence was near and within the actual walls of her home. There would be an infinity of time in the future when she would have leisure, far too much leisure, to see slowly, completely and clearly, and she dreaded the hollowness of the hours to come. Now, for the brief space left to them, she only wanted to be the woman Jim wanted her to be. If only she could so compose herself that Jim took back to England the young but more matured image of the girl among the apple trees, then she would have done almost more than was in her power. She lay down on her bed and closed her eyes, and let every muscle and every tendon in her body go limp. For a full five minutes she was absolutely motionless, thinking nothing, hearing nothing, enclosed in a dark cell of silence. Then she got up and started to transform herself into the Marie-Josephe of the morning, and the shadow of her mother as the *châtelaine* of the *Clos d'Argent*.

"You have come to say good-bye to me."

"Yes. The boat sails for England at a quarter-past six and . . . and Marie-Josephe and I are going into the town, into Boulogne." He hesitated. "So I've come to say good-bye and thank you."

"Why do you say 'thank you'?" She smiled. "It is we, all of us, who should say 'thank you' to you. Please stand by the window."

"Of course."

He stood in a shaft of sunshine and looked into the lined, inscrutable face of this elderly French lady, aware that he, too, was being looked upon. Fifty years hence Marie-Josephe would look exactly as her grandmother did today, for into this girl's young flesh had been spilled the same breeding and her young bones had been moulded by the same thumb. He had again that deep sense of human continuity, a sure knowledge of the purpose of God. It was the same bewildering sense, then half-understood and wholly inarticulate, which had sometimes come to him as a boy walking the flanks of the Cotswolds: it was a certainty that all this had happened before and that he, a young boy, walked this grass and these hills in the company of men a thousand years dead, men who had sheltered their strong bodies from the winds with the skins of animals. An ancient courtesy came to him and he said humbly:

"Madame, you will not remember, but when we met today, I kissed your hand."

"I remember very well."

"It's only this." He was suddenly confused. "It's only this, that I'd like you to know that I've never done that before, never in my life."

"I knew that. I said then that you were a *chevalier*. It is true."

He lifted his hands, let them fall.

"Well, I . . . I suppose I'd better go now."

"Yes. You must go. But we will surely meet again. Before you go, there is a question I wish to ask you."

"There is nothing that I will not answer you, Madame."

"That I believe too." She looked him straight in the eyes. "Do you know of a regiment in the British Army, a regiment of men from the West of Ireland, a regiment called 'the Connaught Rangers'?"

"Yes, I do. When I joined in 1939, we had a Troop Sergeant who had served with them in the old days. He was never tired of talking of the Connaught Rangers."

"You make me very happy, Jim. *Au revoir.*"

"Au revoir, Madame."

Marie-Josephe was waiting by the car. Jim frowned. Once again she seemed to have changed, and he was at a loss at first to define the change. Superficially she had again all the frank friendliness of the girl he had met in the *Cimetière de l'Est.* Yet, in an odd way, she appeared to have withdrawn into herself. He had the saddening sense that she had assumed this cloak, this façade, to conceal something, and it distressed him to know that there could be a secret between them. She asked him politely if he would please help her to carry the sack of potatoes for Madame Loget to the car. He looked at her sharply. He had believed that the errand was a fictitious one and that 'Madame Loget' only existed in Marie-Josephe's imagination. She followed the workings of his mind immediately.

"You remember? I explained to Henri that I had to go to Madame Loget and that a sack of potatoes would not look very nice in his beautiful car."

"Yes. Of course I remember. But I had the impression that——"

"Your impression was not a true one. You do not know me very well. I never tell stories."

"Sorry, Marie-Josephe. I'm sorry. I'm an ass."

"No. Not a donkey. But if you knew me better, you would not believe that I make up stories."

"I apologise. And now, let me give you a lift with the spuds."

"The spuds?"

"Potatoes."

"Of course. I forgot the word, but I know it quite well."

It was his turn. He said guilelessly:

"A moment ago you said that you never told stories."

She laughed and her reserve vanished like mist before the sun.

"I only tell stories about small things, like concerning 'spuds'."

"Spuds and 'spreaders'."

"And possibly about 'spreaders'. Never about big things. There, in the corner, is the sack of . . . of spuds."

"Were you going to carry that sack all the way to the car by yourself?"

"Why not? I am quite strong. It may not be very elegant for a lady to be strong, but I will show you."

"You'll do no such thing."

It was a great satisfaction for him to carry the great weight on his back, and when he slid it off his shoulders into the Renault, he was sweating. Absent-mindedly he wiped his forehead with Marie-Josephe's handkerchief.

"That is mine?"

He looked at it with acute embarrassment and stammered. "Yes. I'm afraid it is. S—s—sorry. I meant to give it back to you, but I forgot."

"Did you?" There was a flash of laughter in her dark eyes and he distinctly saw a quiver at the corner of her mouth. "Perhaps it would be better if you were to guard, to keep it—for use after carrying sacks of . . . spuds." She put her head on one side. "Do you consider that the thing to start the car with will still work?"

"I hope so. Of course, your battery's pretty down. We'll try."

When he pressed the self-starter, the engine gave a feeble groan. He jumped out of the car again and went to the front. "Damn. You'd better get in and I'll wind. You pull out a thing called the choke, and if you tell me that you know the word 'choke', I frankly won't believe you. Ready."

"I am ready. And I do know what the 'choke' is. It is English for a funny story. What we here in France call *'une blague'*."

He said, shaking his head:

"Sometimes I think you must be 'une blague' yourself,

Marie-Josephe, for it is hard to believe that you are as you are—and true."

"Oh yes. I am quite true. Would you like to drive this splendid motor-car? If you say 'yes', it is necessary for me to remind you that this is France and not England. One drives to the right. *Tenez à droite.* Also, if you drive, you will please remember that this is a motor-car. It is not a tank and you are no longer a sergeant."

"I told your fiancé that this afternoon, that I was no longer a sergeant."

"My fiancé?" She waved a sunburned hand, dismissing the word. "My fiancé. Oh, of course. You desire to drive this magnificent carriage?"

"No. You drive."

"You are prepared to trust yourself with me?"

He looked at her, standing by the open door of the car, one white sandalled foot on the rusty running-board. His heart missed a beat.

"Yes, Marie-Josephe. I am prepared to do that."

Her eyebrows rose, and he was sure that he saw again the glimmer of laughter at the corner of her mouth and under her lashes.

"You are . . . quite sure?"

"Quite sure, Marie-Josephe."

She shrugged, smiling.

"This is most flattering. For what may now happen, I take no responsibility. *Allons-y!*"

"What does that mean?"

"It means, Jim, that like your 25th Lancers, we are going to press on regardless."

"*Allons-y,*" said Jim.

The same road, dark between cool forests of pine; the same goats in the grass, the same buttercups; telegraph posts, snatching handfuls of shimmering wires from the sky and flinging them to each other, seen through the same cracked windscreen; the needle on the dashboard shivering as the battery collected strength. It was all sharply familiar to Jim. The dome of the Cathedral beckoned them to the huddle of the town, and beyond the town stretched the sea, and beyond the sea were the far-away cliffs of Kent.

"Jim."

"Yes."

"I have remarked that you are beginning to speak French very well. I could teach you quite soon to speak it like a true *Boulonnais.* Then we could have long conversations about spuds and spreaders and . . . and heifers and the English prophet Daniel, and we could speak in which language we wished, English or French. Would you like that?"

"Very much. What's French for a spreader?"

She hadn't the faintest idea. She said with composure:

"Ah! That is too difficult a word for you. Much too difficult. Relate to me one thing. When you went to say good-bye to Grandmère, she spoke to you in English?"

"Yes. Shall I—relate to you what she said?"

"Please."

"She told me a lot of stories about you when you were a little girl and how wicked you were and how you used to pretend that you knew things quite well when you didn't know them at all. Then she asked me an odd thing. She asked me if I had ever heard of a regiment called the Connaught Rangers."

"And had you?"

"Quite by chance I had. When I first joined up in '39, my Troop Sergeant was an Irishman and he'd served with them years and years ago, before they were disbanded. He wore their cap-badge in his beret at Alamein. He was killed wearing it, and we buried him still wearing it. We liked him very much."

"Grandmère—was she pleased that you knew of this regiment?"

"I think she was very pleased. I don't know why."

"I too am glad. And I do know why." She drove on in silence. Then she said in a small voice, looking straight ahead. "Have you noticed anything, Jim?"

"I've noticed so many things, the sort of things that I've never noticed before in anybody. May I tell you some of them?"

"Oh yes. Please."

He tried to sort his thoughts out, to put them coherently. He was surprised at the ease with which he spoke to a woman, using the sort of uninhibited expressions which, a few hours ago, would have been far beyond his compass.

"You are so many different persons—and you keep on

adding to the list of these strange ladies. I told you that already, but since then you have confronted me with at least two more variations of Marie-Josephe. By the barley, after you'd talked to your Monsieur Dubot, you were as taut as piano-wire. Now you aren't any longer. And yet you're different from the girl you were in the *Cimetière de l'Est.* I don't know what goes on inside you, and I believe that it would take me a thousand years to find out. But I can tell you how you're outwardly different."

"Please tell."

"If I use the wrong words, you will have to forgive me because I don't know about women's clothes."

"Please continue."

"Right. Here goes. When I saw you this morning, you were wearing a cotton dress or frock. It was white with clusters of flowers on it, coloured flowers. You had no stockings, no hat and you wore sandals. You were much smaller than me, and when you spoke you had to look up. That's how I know about the sandals. And you were also wearing the medal that I remembered. Am I right so far?"

"Quite right. It is possibly not very polite of you to remark that I wore no stockings, but then the English are not very —I don't know the word—*mondain.*"

"It means sophisticated, worldly."

"Ah yes. Of course."

"You knew the word all the time—naturally?"

"But naturally. Please do not mock yourself of me."

"Sorry." He half-smiled. It was unnecessary for him even to glance at her, so clear was her image in his mind. "Now the only thing that remains the same is the medal. You are now wearing a dress of green silk. You have on white sandals, but these ones have heels. That I know because when you faced me in the yard I was not much taller than you. You looked up a bit, but not much. Also—forgive my unworldliness—but you are now wearing stockings and a little more lipstick than you did this morning. Also your hair is different. You are the same girl, but you have added a measure of elegance." He turned and looked at her, his grey eyes alight. "Admit that I am a most observant man."

She sighed.

"That I cannot admit with truth. I think you may be observant about things that are of small importance, but in big things you are blind. Possibly your eyes will come to you later. I hope so very much."

Already they had reached the outskirts of Boulogne. Marie-Josephe went on.

"First we will go to the house of Madame Loget and leave there the spuds. When you have helped me to put the sack in the hall of the house, I will ask you to await me in the car. If I were to present you to her, she would wish to prepare tea with lemon in the English manner and have a long conversation with you. And there is another place where we must go."

They had reached the *Grande Rue* and its crowded pavements and its busy shops, and Marie-Josephe turned to the right into the *rue Dosille*. With some difficulty, Jim got the sack of potatoes from the back and stood it upright inside the door of Madame Loget's house. Marie-Josephe said that she would be five minutes at most. Jim sat down in the car and lit a cigarette.

He looked at his watch. In just under two hours the boat would sail for England and he would be on board. In under two hours, the propellers would start churning and the distance between him and this girl would lengthen with every surge of the sea. There would be many explanations to be made to The Hand and Flower Darts Club. Where had he been all day and why hadn't he turned up? Had he been in trouble with the Frenchies? He smiled. He could almost hear Mr. Collins speaking. "Now, Jim, I would rather tear my tongue out than enquire into other people's business but . . ." And Charley. Charley would have no doubts at all as to how Jim had spent his day . . . nor would Shorty. The only person he would be glad to see again would be Luke Grenfell. He wouldn't mind a bit talking to Luke.

Marie-Josephe came out of Madame Loget's house and got into the car. She said:

"I was a very long time?"

"Hours and hours. I was thinking about my friends and what I would say to them when we meet again at the boat."

"And what will you say?"

"To one of them, I will say that I met you. The others would only make 'chokes' about you, so they can go and fish."

"Suppose they do not want to fish."

"They'll have to fish, all the same. Where are we going now?"

"We are going to the place that the man in the shop where they give away roses told you to go. It is not far away from here, and after that we will, if you like, search for your friends."

"I'll see them soon enough."

"Is there still nothing that you have noticed, Jim?"

"I've noticed lots of things. I've noticed a thousand things."

"But not one thing, one special thing?"

He shook his head, mystified.

"Please tell me what it is."

"No. You must find out for yourself."

After the white sunshine of the streets, the vaulted spaces of the Cathedral were dim and cool. A circle of candles burned steadily before the Hand of Our Lady of Boulogne, and the water into which Marie-Josephe slid the tips of her fingers was tepid to his touch. It was curious to hear the heels of her sandals tap-tapping on the tiled floor, and to follow her and to see her genuflect deeply. He did it too, copying her movements exactly. He walked after her up the aisle towards the high altar and he knelt when she knelt. He supposed that he'd better pray as well.

It was a long time since he had addressed himself to God, but the long-familiar phrases, etched for ever in his mind, came back readily enough, and he repeated them in silence, trying for the first time in his life to translate these well-worn patterns of sound into living words with meaning. He tried in vain. It was not possible for him suddenly to precipitate himself into a mood of contemplation when his mind was so sensitive to the presence of the girl who knelt beside him. In spite of this, it was with great tranquillity that he gazed through his fingers at the high altar.

Between tall candles, Our Lady sat in the bows of a fishing-boat, holding the Infant in her arms. Mother and Child were crowned with gold. There was a simplicity, a calmness, about their attitude that Jim found strangely significant, and it occurred to him that no tempest could ever rock that boat or even ruffle the draperies of its precious cargo. He glanced at Marie-Josephe. She, too, had finished the formulæ of prayer, and she was looking steadily at the altar, her face cupped in her hands. Without at first realising its import, he noticed that there was a little pale circle at the base of one of her sunburned fingers, as if this one place had hitherto been shielded from the strength of the sun. He was kneeling at her left and the hand that he saw was her left hand. She turned her face away from the altar, and looked at him with that candid glance he was beginning to know and to love. He put his strong hand between them and opened his fingers. Her hand slid into his hand, and he contained it in his, holding it strongly, touching with incredulous fingers the pale circle where Henri's ring had been.

CHAPTER SEVENTEEN

"Englishmen have two left arms."
RIVAROL (according to Anatole France)

ONE by one, the members of The Hand and Flower Darts Club, who had gone their several ways on their several missions, began to consider moving in the general direction of the Etoile. The sun had passed its zenith and Mr. Collins's summons to congregate at five o'clock, come what may, had been categoric. Like trencher-fed hounds who had gaily hunted their own lines over the afternoon, they harked leisurely back to the huntsman's horn.

But not Shorty.

When he saw that Luke Grenfell was engrossed in a French book that hadn't even got any pictures in it, he supposed that he'd better pretend to read something too. His eye was caught by a brightly coloured cover. It was a cheap edition of a work entitled *Pour l'Amour d'un Légionnaire,* and Shorty looked at it with unaccountable excitement. The designer of the cover had let himself go. The sun descended in glory behind a frieze of date-palms, and beyond the silhouette of the palms stretched the illimitable distances of the Sahara. In the foreground a soldier in a blue uniform with a white cloak bent passionately over an Arab lady whose protection against the night air consisted largely of a pair of ear-rings, a diaphanous kilt and some bangles. There was little doubt as to the soldier's intentions and even less as to the Arab lady's powers of resistance. Shorty looked at the soldier for a long time. Proper tall chap. Must be a good six feet—if not more. Some people got all the luck. He nudged Luke Grenfell. He said accusingly:

"You speak French, Lukey-boy."

"I also speak English. Luke's my name. Not 'Lukey-boy'."

"All right, all right, all right. You call me 'Shorty'. No offence meant. What's this mean?"

Luke took the book from Shorty, and looked at it much as a bacteriologist might look at a particularly repellent bacillus.

"It means 'For the love of a Legionnaire'."

"And what's a 'Legionnaire'?"

"Chap in the Foreign Legion. Easy."

"Like Ronald Colman?"

Luke frowned.

"Like who?"

"Ronald Colman. Film star. I suppose you got to be pretty tall to get into the Foreign Legion?"

"I'm afraid I don't know their minimum requirements. I think they like 'em tough rather than tall. What was your friend's name again?"

"Ronald Colman. Did you never see 'Beau Geste'?"

Luke shook his head.

"No. I must confess that 'Beau Geste', alas, is one of the films that escaped me."

"It was smashing," said Shorty.

So they liked them tough in the Foreign Legion, did they? Shorty took a deep breath so that his chest swelled to straining point and he tightened every muscle in his body. He was so tough that he could shave with a blow-lamp, so tough that he could drink water and spit rust. What the hell was he waiting for?

"Luke."

"Yes, Shorty."

"Suppose a bloke wanted to join the Foreign Legion, what would he do?"

"Heavens, I don't know." He smiled. "When in doubt, ask a policeman."

"Ask a copper. Coo!"

Coppers were Shorty's natural enemies. Coppers put their hands firmly on Shorty's shoulder and said, "Come along, you"; coppers stood in the witness-box and intoned . . . "Your Worship, I was on duty in Belsize Road at 10.15 a.m. on Tuesday, the 24th of November, keeping observation on the accused man. . . ."

Shorty looked out into the sunny street. A French policeman in riding breeches and a revolver was directing the traffic with a whistle and a white baton. This was a copper and he carried a gun. At least English coppers didn't carry guns. Shorty shrank instinctively. He had a moment of complete panic, and then, with a great effort, he controlled the quivering in his knees. He looked again at the lurid cover of the book. Sun . . . date-palms . . . and a uniform like Ronald Colman—instead of rain, doorways, coppers and Mr. McIsaac.

Of course, they mightn't take him, not a chap of his size . . . but at least he'd have a bash at it. He glanced at Luke Grenfell, who was still engrossed in his reading. Soundlessly he whispered, "Cheerio, Lukey-boy, and thanks for the tip."

He escaped death in the traffic by a hair's breadth. The policeman saluted him with ironic courtesy:

"*Vous désirez, Monsieur?*"

"Speak English?"

"A liddle."

"Listen, Copper," said Shorty breathlessly, "can you tell me where to go to join the Foreign Legion?"

Général Felix de la Chanterelle, even *en civille,* was a striking figure. Officier de la Légion d'Honneur, Medaille Militaire, Croix de Guerre avec Palme, Grand Cross of the Most Exalted Order of Saint Dominic, Chevalier du Nicham Iftikhar, Distinguished Service Order, Burgess of Boulogne, he wore one black eyeglass and a vast moustache with twisted ends. The panama hat which he swept off on entering the café revealed a stiff crop of grey hair. A pearl-and-emerald tiepin gleamed in his black cravat, his tussore suit was pressed with military precision, his white buckskin shoes were like fresh-fallen snow, and the silver-topped walking-stick was in itself an emblem of authority. No frequenter of cafés, he had admittedly lunched without due discretion, and now found it necessary to enter a public place on the most humble of human missions. By doing so, he blithely set in motion the sequence of events which were to trundle from comedy to catastrophe, from the ludicrous to the lewd.

The General laid his panama hat and stick on a table, rapped out an order for coffee and marched to the same swing doors through which Pierre Jumelle had vanished not sixty seconds ago. Trevor Hilgrove watched him idly. He supposed the old boy was going to use the telephone. But suppose he wasn't going to use the telephone . . . Suppose . . .

Trevor sat up with a jerk. It was vital, absolutely vital, that he should be the next person after Pierre to enter that discreet hide-out. He crushed out his cigarette, grabbed his dart-board, crossed the room like a panther and launched himself through the swing doors.

He stopped short in a small paved ante-room. Two doors confronted him, one shut and one open. The shut one had over it the word *'Messieurs'* and the lock on the door was turned to *'Occupé'*. The other door, marked *'Dames'*, swung invitingly open. With one white buckskin shoe tapping impatiently on the tiled floor, Général de la Chanterelle waited. Trevor Hilgrove leaned against the wall. The General eyed him with fierce disfavour. There was a moment's pregnant silence. Then the General spoke stiffly:

"Monsieur, j'attends."

Innate courtesy struggled with the General's physical preoccupation and won the day.

"You are English?"

"Yes."

"Ah. The English are always welcome in Boulogne." He managed a painful smile. "But you understand, Monsieur, I wait. It is I who was first 'ere. You will return later, yes?"

"No."

"But, Monsieur——"

"Listen," said Trevor easily, "why don't you use that one? It's free."

Thirty seconds passed before the General understood. His face was suddenly brick-red and it seemed as if he were fighting for breath. He said, when he could speak:

"You suggest that I, *Général de France,* should employ, make use of, a cabinet reserved for the ladies?"

"Why not? It's free."

The General's eye-glass dropped out of his eye, swung on its black ribbon. As his chest swelled, his English fled. With great self-control, he managed to confine himself to one phrase:

"Dégoûttant personnage!"

The lock on the door slid from *'Occupé'* to *'Libre'*, and Pierre, his part of Operation Timepiece accomplished, emerged. He looked neither to the right nor the left as he passed through the swing doors—*en route* for the railway-station and for Paris. Like greyhounds released simultaneously from adjacent traps, Général de la Chanterelle and Trevor Hilgrove leapt for the narrow door. Their shoulders met and locked. For all his years the General was the more agile, Trevor a shade the broader. Their determination was exactly equal. Trevor appeared to relax painfully for a split second. The General glanced at him in sudden concern. This was Trevor's chance. With a mighty heave of his shoulder, he sent the General, momentarily off his guard, reeling back against the telephone bracket, darted inside and slammed the door. The lock snapped derisively from *'Libre'* to *'Occupé'* and Général de la Chanterelle realised that he had been outwitted. He counter-attacked with vigour and fury.

As Trevor stood on the seat and groped behind the cistern, a positive fusillade of blows and kicks sounded on the door and he could distinguish some of the General's richer expletives. *"Crapaud! Espèce de Satyr! Saligaud!"* Ah well, hard words broke no bones. He shouted, "Oh, do shut up. I won't be long." He immediately found what he sought, the square brown paper parcel left by Pierre. From his pocket he whipped a small screwdriver and, sitting down, unscrewed the front of his dart-board. It lifted off easily, for Trevor had spent an hour practising this very operation overnight in London. Inside was a circular hollow space, lined with cotton-wool. He opened the brown-paper parcel and the cardboard box it contained. Inside, gleaming dully in the electric light, lay some fifty tiny gold wrist-watches. With skilful fingers, Trevor began to place the watches one by one on the cotton-wool inside the dart-board. . . .

Outside in the ante-chamber, the General measured the distance from the wall to the door with his one good eye. It was about two and a half metres. If one were to crouch against the wall and suddenly fling oneself with all one's force against the door, it is possible that the lock would break. Muttering, he took off his jacket and folded it to use as a shoulder-pad. His digestive discomfort had passed away completely, and he was only possessed of a cold fury for victory. He rolled up his sleeves. He sank down on his haunches and was just bracing his muscles for the charge when the swing door to the café opened and a sedate, middle-aged woman entered the ante-chamber. In spite of her flowered straw hat and fur tippet, it was with horror that Général de la Chanterelle recognised his cook on her afternoon out.

She gaped at him. Slowly he rose to an erect position. Her mouth opened and shut. With what dignity he could muster, the General rolled down his sleeves, put on his jacket and shot his cuffs. He bowed as if to a stranger.

"Passez, Madame."

"Mais, Monsieur le Général, je . . . je——"

"J'ai dit 'passez, Madame'," he said sharply. *"Ca suffit."*

With many a backward glance, the unfortunate woman

entered the free compartment. The lock slid to *'Occupé'* Général de la Chanterelle looked at the two uncompromising doors and gritted his teeth.

It took Trevor Hilgrove a good five minutes to transfer the precious contraband to its hiding-place and to screw the two halves of the dart-board so tightly together that no join was visible. Trevor supposed that the old boy outside must have gone away. Not that it mattered. He disposed of the now empty cardboard box and the crumpled brown paper, tucked the dart-board under his arm and opened the door.

Nemesis in a black eyeglass was standing stiffly against the wall. There was something terribly ominous in the General's immobility and in his silence, and Trevor half backed into the *cabinet*. He began to say "Sorry I was so long, old chap," but the words stuck in his throat. The General bowed frigidly and handed Trevor a visiting-card. He took it mechanically and read it:

Général Felix de la Chanterelle,
Grand Officier de la Legion d'Honneur.
31 Boulevard Louis Hérault
Boulogne-sur-Mer.

Trevor gulped. He managed a weak but winning smile.

"I'm most awfully sorry to have kept you waiting, Sir. I can only apologise. Honestly, Sir. . . ."

The electric light gleamed on the General's black eyeglass and on his one unblinking eye. Trevor shifted his feet.

"I 'ave presented my card. I await your card . . . Sir."

"But do listen. I've said that I'm terribly sorry. . . ."

"I await your card, Sir."

Trevor stared at him, erect, stocky, proud. There was nothing else for it. Anyway, what the hell? After a moment he shrugged and felt in his waistcoat pocket. His fingers encountered a slip of pasteboard given him that very morning by the quayside tout, and he had difficulty in suppressing a grin. He produced it with an air. The General took it. Trevor bowed. Discretion was clearly the better part of valour, and his feet were eager for the fresh air and the pavements of the *place Robespierre*. Clutching his highly precious dart-board to his chest, he walked quickly through the *Café Gérard* and between the twin bay trees into the street. All was still well with Operation Timepiece. . . .

Alone in the ante-room, Général de la Chanterelle looked at the card. He frowned. It was not possible! It could not be possible. With his one incredulous eye he read:

MAURICE SEVRIER
Taxis: All informations:
English spokken: Specialities.

Despite his third rebuff, Charley Brewer was still undeterred in his determination to shape his day into the form that he had foreseen. France was France. Trouble was, it was getting late. . . . There was nobody much about, so he decided to take the weight off his plates-of-meat for a minute or two. He sat down on the pavement, his back against the wall, and began to fan himself with his bowler hat. From this point of vantage he was able to look down the road and observe in detail the solitary figure approaching. Hope, long deferred, rose sharply at the sight of the gentleman's white shoes, somewhat flamboyant tiepin and Albert watch-chain. These attributes, together with a luxuriant moustache, were possessed in some measure by Charley himself, and led him into the fatal error of hailing the stranger as a blood-brother. Noting the black eyeglass and the martial carriage, Charley was reassured. Ah well, here we go. Soldiers all. . . .

He scrambled to his feet and, sweeping off his bowler hat with a low bow, accosted the stranger.

Général Felix de la Chanterelle, although still seething at his recent encounter with the British, was at heart of a cordial nature and accustomed to private soldiers. He said guardedly:

"*Bonjour, mon vieux.*"

"Speak English, Chum?"

The general started as if he had been stung. He recoiled sharply. He hesitated, torn between his normal good nature and the desire to remove himself from further contamination by the unspeakable islanders. He compromised by saying bleakly:

"Non. No Engleesh."

Careering blindly to his downfall, Charley plunged into the foreign lingo. He sidled up to the General's ear and said hoarsely:

"*Je voo un femme.*"

"*Quoi? Vous avez faim?*" The General softened momentarily. "You are 'ungry?"

"No, Chum. Not 'ungry." He winked. "Leastways, not except for one thing."

Unsuspecting and anxious to make his wishes perfectly clear, Charley began to illustrate with lavish and unmistakable gestures. He had only half finished his impersonation of the feminine torso when history repeated itself. The General's black eyeglass had dropped and he was again fighting for breath. By the time Charley had completed the picture, the General was in full voice. He had a wide vocabulary, but his splendid flow of invective was unheard by Charley, whose nimble gym shoes were once again fleeing from disaster.

This time Charley did not have to run far.

Maurice Sevrier, guide to Boulogne and self-appointed purveyor of taxis, informations and *spécialités*, came upon him almost at once. Charley was leaning against the wall of a chemist's shop. He had had time to catch his breath, and was moodily playing 'It's love that makes the world go round' on his mouth-organ. Maurice Sevrier brightened a little. This one, this solitary one, would surely be ignorant of the various denominations of franc notes. And he had seen him before, coming off the boat. Then he had been guarded by his friends. Now he was alone—and therefore defenceless. Of course, the likelihood was that he had already spent all his money, but that one could soon find out. Somewhat wearily, he adjusted his routine smile and lifted his peaked cap.

"*Bonjour, Milord.*"

" 'Ullo," said Charley morosely, "you again."

"But yes." He laughed heartily as if Charley had just made an excellent joke. " 'Ere we are—like the bad penny. You 'ave 'ad a good time in Boulogne, yes?"

"No I 'aven't," said Charley. "Everything's been a proper muck-up."

"You 'ave bought seelk stockings, *parfum, cartes postales*, everything?"

"No. Bought nothing yet. I don't seem to get the hang of the money 'ere."

A wolfish look came into Maurice's eyes.

"You got all your money left . . . *Milord*?"

"Sure. Got plenty of dough."

" 'Ow much?" Maybe the question had been asked too quickly, for Maurice saw a gleam of suspicion in Charley's eye. He went on with a careless laugh. "Not that it matter. I 'ave many friends, all English people. All English people 'oo come to Boulogne know me and have confidence. English lords, ladies, sirs, all sorts."

Charley played a few bars of 'Knees up Mother Brown', and suddenly broke off. " 'Member when I saw you this morning at the boat?"

Maurice was suddenly alert.

"Yes."

" 'Member you said you knew some sort of café place——"

"Ah. *Chez Poupette*. It is always very gay. Laughing, singing, dancing, all sorts——"

"All sorts?" said Charley meaningly. "You're quite sure about the all sorts?"

"Monsieur," said Maurice with dignity, "I, personally, absolutely guarantee. As a 'onourable gentleman, I guarantee—all sorts."

" 'Ow much would it cost?" said Charley with caution.

" 'Ow much 'ave you got . . . *Milord*?"

"That much!"

With a practised eye Maurice analysed and assessed the bundle in Charley's hand. Supper was assured at last and, with luck, tomorrow's breakfast as well. . . . He said briskly:

"O-Kay. We go to *Chez Poupette*."

"You're quite sure," said Charley. "I've 'ad one or two setbacks already today."

"I 'ave said that as 'onourable gentleman, I guarantee."

Charley slid his mouth-organ into his breast pocket and blew his nose.

"Come on," he said.

Their steps led them in the direction of the harbour. In the devastation of broken houses, one row had remained more or less intact. It contained a ship-chandlers, an antique shop, a bicycle shop—and *Chez Poupette*. From within the bead curtains came the sound of a gramophone and Charley's pace quickened. Home at last. . . .

"You called me Baby Doll a year ago,
You told me I was very nice to know . . ."

whined the gramophone.

"*Entrez*," said Maurice grandly—and held back the bead curtains.

Within, all was frolic, feast and fun.

Mr. Fred Collins, licensee of The Hand and Flower, stared with haggard, imploring eyes at the ceiling. He was praying with all his strength that no member of the Darts Club should happen that way, for the lady with the glass ear-rings was sitting on the lap of his best trousers and one of her angular arms was clamped round his neck. A half-empty bottle of sweet champagne that Mr. Collins hadn't even ordered stood on the table beside them and the gramophone whined incessantly. As a result of her aged playfulness, Mr. Collins's solitary quiff of hair was twirled perpendicularly upwards from his forehead, there was a perfect imprint of her mouth in lipstick on his left cheek and—for reasons only known to herself—she had skittishly unlaced one of his boots. For the hundredth time, Mr. Collins failed to understand what sudden madness had impelled him to answer the gramophone's siren call—and how this unspeakable harridan had managed to insinuate herself on to his knee. He took a deep, shuddering breath and once again attempted vainly to remove her constricting arm.

"Listen," he said hoarsely, "I got to go."

For answer, Poupette leaned forward and bit the lobe of his ear with her false teeth. She said languorously:

"Naughtee boy!"

It was at this untimely juncture that the bead curtains were drawn back and that the Captain of The Hand and Flower Darts Club strode purposefully into *Chez Poupette.*

Charley stopped dead.

The anticipatory grin on his face was slowly replaced by a look of utter incredulity. His mouth gaped. Avenging Angel in a bowler hat, he stared blankly at the wilting licensee of The Hand and Flower. The look of unbelief gave way to one of pious outrage. Charley had had little practise in this particular expression, and he gave to it all the freshness of the amateur. After an infinity of time, he shook his head in deep and shocked reproof.

"Mr. Collins," said Charley Brewer the coalman, " 'ow could you?"

CHAPTER EIGHTEEN

Jim Carver stood beside Marie-Josephe on the steps of the Cathedral, looking out over the cobbled street. He had put a lot of money, he didn't know how much, into a collecting-box for the poor, and he felt at last that he had really given the roses to George Holden. The secret which had been revealed to him in the candle-lit gloom of the church had become an acute embarrassment to him in the blinding daylight, and both he and Marie-Josephe were without words. A mongrel dog came to them, and Marie-Josephe bent down and began to stroke it, talking to it with great animation. Unfortunately it didn't stay long, and when it scampered away to sniff in the dustbins, they watched it go with intense, absorbed regret, as if they had lost a friend. Marie-Josephe said with an effort:

"He was a very nice dog, wasn't he?"

"Yes. Very. But he wasn't a he. He was a she."

"Oh yes. I didn't notice. I wonder what was her name."

"Might be anything."

"Yes. Naturally. It might be Fi-fi—or anything. Do you prefer this dog to Siki?"

"No, no. I much prefer Siki. Much."

"I also. Although Siki is a savage dog with those who are not his friends, I prefer him to this dog."

Jim said lamely:

"When I was a boy and I lived in the country, I had a lurcher. His name was Jip and he was a great one for hunting rabbits."

"What is a 'lurcher'? Is it also a dog?"

"Yes. It's a cross between a——" He shrugged. "Well, it's a sort of cross."

"Of course. I had forgotten the word. 'Lurcher'. I knew of course that you were of the country because you had knowledge of boules and of our barley. But this . . . this Hand and Flower is in London, is it not?"

"Yes. It's in Saint John's Wood. You see, I work in London, but I actually come from the country." He sighed. "From the Cotswolds, from over beyond Burford."

"This Burford, is it an English city?"

"No. Indeed no." He laughed, glad to be laughing. "Burford is far from being a city. It's a small, old town, one of the sheep towns, with a steep hill and a church where Cromwell's men stabled their horses. You can see the halter-chains to this day. At the bottom of the hill, there's a river called the Windrush, and in it there are trout and crayfish and eels and jack-pike." Remembering his boyhood, the ghost of a Cotswold accent manifested itself in his words. "I used to have an eel-trap in the Windrush, over beyond Upton, and many's the pheasant I took from the Priory Woods." He paused. How strange it was to be standing with Marie-Josephe looking over French cobbles and seeing with his eyes French names of the shops—things like *Bijouterie* and *Epicerie*—when with his vision he was looking at the bright ripples of the Windrush. How strange to stand on the steps of a French Cathedral when he was really crouched behind a wall of Cotswold stone, waiting to see the hares start up and run and frolic on the frosty grass in the spring moonlight. Proper playful they were, the hares. . . .

"Why are you smiling, Jim?"

"I'm thinking of the hares in the Cotswolds and the games they get up to."

"The hares?" She brushed her fingers through her own dark hair and he smiled.

"No. Not hairs like that. Hares with long ears, like this."

"Oh, of course. I am very stupid. In French, the word is *lièvre,* and we have many hares here. It is most exciting to see them play among themselves and dance. It is like a ballet."

He glanced at her. She too was smiling. Looking at Marie-Josephe, the sea that lay between France and England seemed to shrink, and the fields of the two countries to join so that the hares would have more room to drum and gambol in the shared moonlight. He said slowly:

"No. It is I who am the stupid one. I didn't realise that you have hares here, too."

"But naturally. Have you never heard of *civet de lièvre*? It is quite delicious." She went on absently, the glimmer of a smile moving one corner of her mouth. "I would very much like sometime to cook it for you, on cold nights, with a bottle of red wine on the hearth and the wind outside——"

She stopped, aghast. Her hand flew to the guilty corner of her mouth. She was appalled by what she had said and by what she had done. Deliberately over the last hour, she had driven all thought of the future into the back of her mind, holding it there behind a screen of words about anything, about nothing. Suddenly, painfully, the screen had been ripped open to reveal the bleeding tissue beneath. Without thinking, she had made articulate the image of her desire, and she had said this dreadful thing out loud. She had said it simply and without guile. But she had used a phrase that she had no right to use, and she was horrified at its implication. So absorbed had she become with herself and the magnitude of what she had done that she had clean forgotten—or caused herself to forget—the very existence of anyone cast in a shape approximating to her own who could have any claim on the man who stood beside her. Yet such a person did exist, unknown and thereby the more menacing. What would she be like, this English lady who would one day be the bride of Sergeant Jim Carver of the 25th Lancers? Marie-Josephe's knowledge of English ladies was meagre. What was the phrase he had used, it must be a thousand years ago? He had said that she was young, young and fair and very pretty. 'Young' was a word that meant nothing, for the English ladies, because of their fresh, rain-washed skins, were as ageless as their own damp island. She lived in London, this Mademoiselle Cherry Mitchell, therefore, because she lived in the capital of England, she would not only be pretty but elegant as well. She would be tall and blonde with an incurving spine, and with the self-assurance that comes to women who inhabit capital cities. How often had she seen these women, these *produits d'Angleterre,* coming down the gangways of the steamers from England, stepping disdainfully over the cobbles on narrow shoes made of crocodile skin, towards the Paris train, going from the pavements of one capital to the *boulevards* of another? To Marie-Josephe they had been creatures from the mists, dehumanised creatures from a world without work or trouble or anxiety, these visitors who were bravely prepared to face the ordeal of France with a thermos of tea, this week's *Punch* and several tins of disinfectant. They were not real women of whom one might ever be jealous. My faith, no! One might as well be jealous of the effigy of . . . of Jeanne d'Arc in the waxworks at

Rouen. It would be equally absurd.

But Mademoiselle Cherry Mitchell was one of this tweedy sisterhood. In a flash the whole tailored brood, hitherto remote, had become human and dangerous and objects of a fierce, new-found jealousy—with Cherry Mitchell as the immediate target. She would wear a small hat with the lances of Jim's regiment on it in diamonds. She would have slender hips and she would carry a shoulder-bag, and she would, of course, wear gloves to cover her beautiful, useless hands. Marie-Josephe glanced at her own, trembling, sunburned fingers. They belonged to the hands of one who could hack bracken, they belonged to one who could drive a straight furrow before the picking, screaming gulls, they were the fingers that Jim had clasped strongly—in the presence of Our Lady. As for Mademoiselle Cherry Mitchell . . . *que le diable l'emporte,* might the devil fly away with her, her diamond clip, her thermos of tea and her tins of disinfectant, and might he deposit the lot in the innermost cavern of hell. . . .

Marie-Josephe took a step backwards. So sudden and so violent had been her emotion that her knees had turned to water and she had difficulty in breathing. She half-leaned and half-sat on the old stone balustrade. When she spoke at last, every shred of warmth had gone from her voice, and Jim knew with dismay that yet another Marie-Josephe had come to bewilder the scurrying hours left to them.

"Of course, I do not mean that at all." She gave a tiny, brittle laugh. "My English is not good and I make foolish mistakes."

"What did you mean?"

"Oh, that is quite easy. I wished to say that I would write down for you on a piece of paper the method, the manner in which we in France prepare *civet de lièvre,* so that you can give this piece of paper to your fiancée, to Mademoiselle Mitchell. She will then be able to cook it for you on cold nights, with a bottle of red wine—or is it not the practice of the English to drink whisky?—with a bottle of whisky on the hearth and the wind outside, the English wind. That is what I wished to say."

He took a swift, troubled step towards her and put his two hands on her shoulders.

"I don't believe you."

"Oh." Her eyebrows rose. "Is it the custom in England for men to say to ladies that they do not speak the truth?"

"I don't know about other men or their customs. I only know about myself and I say it to you."

"You know about yourself? How very fortunate you are! I have often wished to know about myself. It is possibly a presumption on the part of the daughter of a farmer from Boulogne to consider that she is in any respect worthy of self-analysis. I have just decided that my power of expression in English is remarkable for the daughter of a farmer—even if you consider that she uses her knowledge to speak things which are not true. Will you please take your hands from my shoulders?"

Her flesh was resistant under the pressure of his muscular fingers.

"Do you want me to?"

"Yes. No." She laughed. "It is as you wish. It affects me not at all. But it cannot please you to put your hands upon the shoulders of one whom you believe to be a *menteuse*, one who does not speak the truth."

In the quiet afternoon he heard from inside the Cathedral the soft chiming of bells. When that little soothing sound had lost itself, he spoke with great deliberation.

"It pleases me very much. It would please me even more to take you into my arms on a cold night, with the wind outside. Do you hear and understand what I say to you, Marie-Josephe?"

She heard—and she understood. Though these were the words she ardently wanted to hear, the fact that he had said them out loud had instantly shattered the crystal bubble of her imagination. She knew with clarity that this was a moment in her life when two courses lay open to her and that she must choose one of the two—now. The decision was hers alone.

What had she done? Over the hours of the day, she had behaved without restraint. She had deliberately encouraged a man whom she had no right to encourage, a man who was already bound in honour to someone else. It was her own monstrous behaviour which had brought her to this position, and it was she who must either plunge more deeply or extricate herself at once. She must advance or retreat. Nothing would be more easy, nothing would give her more delight than to surrender herself wholly to the spell of the day. Fighting every inch of the way, she flung herself into what she considered to be honourable retreat. But it was only by lashing her pride into imagined grievance that she could find strength to do battle with the man she loved. She gave a ripple of laughter.

"Oh, voici des jolies phrases! What pretty things to say! When you return to England tonight, you must place your hands on the shoulders of Mademoiselle Mitchell and say such things to her. It is to her that they belong, *les jolies phrases*. Then, when you have said these pretty things, you can also relate to her of how you met Siki and became at once the master of a savage dog. You can also relate of how you instructed me about a boule, and of how you were made welcome in the farm of my father. It will be most interesting for Mademoiselle Mitchell and together you will have much laughter."

"Marie-Josephe, why have you gone away from me? A few minutes ago, you gave me your hand and there was no ring on it. What does that mean?"

"My ring? Oh, that does not concern you. I have broken my contract with Monsieur Dubot, only for one reason. I have done so because he demanded that I should inform him of the confidences of my Grandmère. It was an impertinence. And I have not gone away. It is impossible for me to go away because you continue to hold my shoulders. You make me your prisoner. This is not a story to relate to Mademoiselle Mitchell. Oh no." She shook her head. "It is of course well understood here in Boulogne that when Englishmen come to France for the day they seek ladies to hold their shoulders. But it would not be understood by Mademoiselle Mitchell. Not at all. She would be jealous. It would be very foolish of her, but she would be jealous, all the same."

"Why, suddenly, do you keep on talking about Cherry?"

"Does it not please you that I should do so? Is it possible that you would like to forget that she exists—for the day? I have sometimes considered that it might be very interesting to be a man and to be able to forget one's responsibilities—for the day. It is less interesting to be a woman, to be the one who is forgotten."

He tried desperately to find the word, the phrase that would bring back the Marie-Josephe who was slipping away from him. But he knew with sadness that there was no word or combination of words that could arrest her flight.

"I don't understand you. I wish I knew where she had gone, the girl who sang '*Savez-vous planter les choux*'?"

"Oh that one! The one in the pinafore who climbed the apple tree the day the tanks went away. She was a foolish little girl and . . . and now she has many new songs. For example, I could sing for you '*J'attendrai*', but it would not be a true song, for it is Mademoiselle Mitchell who awaits you and not I." She drew swiftly backwards so that his hands dropped from her shoulders. With a movement she had broken the last link, the link of his touch, and now there was a space between them. "Please do not think that I have become a stranger. Not at all. You have come to France, and you have been made welcome by those whom you knew when you were one of the liberators of our country. If it had been the privilege of France to have liberated England, we would expect as much." She pretended to consider. "I am not sure if I would regard it as my right to hold one whom I had liberated by the shoulders, but then I am not a man. I am a woman."

He gazed at her, standing facing him, her head a little on one side. She was infinitely desirable, infinitely provocative and as remote as a nun. His reaction was that of a man. A surge of strength flowed along the muscles of his arms and of his shoulders. His fists slowly clenched.

"You deliberately make me aware that you are a woman."

For a split second she swayed where she stood. Then she flung her last reinforcements into the battle, praying that its fury would drive him away now, immediately, before her purpose dissolved in a rising flood of tears.

"You speak like a true Englishman. It is a pity that the cabarets are not open all day, for there you could have found a companion, the sort of person that you desire, instead of wasting your time with the daughter of a farmer. Would you not like me to indicate a gay place where you can spend the little time left to you before you return to that most unfortunate Mademoiselle Mitchell?"

There was nothing left, nothing at all. Looking at her now, at her rigid body and cold, proud face, he knew with bewilderment and dismay that his dream was dispelled and that his day was done. What he did not know was that Marie-

Josephe had suddenly torn down her defences and only wanted him to put out his human hand and draw her strongly into the defeat that lay within his arms. He heard his voice say "Good-bye, Marie-Josephe," and then he turned and walked down the steps of the Cathedral and on blindly down one of the narrow streets towards the bustling town.

Général de la Chanterelle strode along the *Grande Rue,* muttering. He was on his way to the office of his old friend, the Commissaire of Police. The English miscreants would learn that it was no laughing matter to assault and to insult a General of France. They would be sought, these villains, identified, apprehended, charged and punished. Even if it meant combing the town, if it meant holding up the departure of the vessel for England, they would get their deserts. My faith, but yes.

He breasted the hill and crossed the cobbled space before the Cathedral steps. At the corner, a solitary car was standing. As the General passed, he distinctly heard the sound of a woman sobbing. It was no affair of his that a woman should be in tears. He had sterner business to attend to. He had hardly gone a further fifty paces before his march became a walk. Let the foolish creature sit in the car and cry by herself. If one were to attempt to comfort every woman in distress, one would have a busy time. Nevertheless, the General found his walk becoming slower and slower. Finally he stopped. His inborn chivalry struggled with his indignation and won the day. He turned and walked back to the car. It was a battered Renault, and its only occupant was bent over the steering-wheel, her shoulders shaking. With some embarrassment, Général de la Chanterelle took off his panama hat and gave a little cough.

"Pardon, Madame."

The girl in the car lifted a tear-stained face and looked at him. Aha! She was known to him. This was none other than Marie-Josephe, daughter of Louis Berthier, who owned *Clos d'Argent.* But what, in the name of a pipe, was the fiancée of Henri Dubot, doing alone in a car on a Sunday afternoon, and why was she in such distress? The General had no marked affection for Monsieur Dubot, *Notaire,* and if this legal gentleman was responsible for a young girl's tears, he would have little hesitation in laying a stick across his black-gowned shoulders. He said with great sympathy:

"Come, come, child. My name is Général de la Chanterelle, and I am acquainted with your father. This is no way for a charming young lady to be on a sunny afternoon. Will you not permit me to assist you?"

"Nobody can help me. Nobody. And it is all my fault, Monsieur le Général." She wiped her eyes and sniffed. A further outburst of tears was imminent, and the General patted her arm soothingly. She went on in the deepest despair. "It is all my fault because I was stupid and rude, and now he has gone away, I don't know where."

"The permanent departure of Monsieur Dubot," said the General acidly, "is a matter for celebration rather than for tears. There are sweeter fish in the sea than that *requin,* that shark in the coat of a sheep."

"But it is not of Henri Dubot that I speak. I have broken my contract with him. I speak of Jim Carver."

"Of whom?"

"Of Jim. Of Jim Carver of the Lancers, the 25th Lancers."

The General drew in breath with a little hiss.

"He is English, this man who causes you to cry?"

"Yes. English. He is from . . . from over beyond Burford in . . . the Cotswolds in England."

Général de la Chanterelle opened the door of the car and stood as straight as a ramrod. His moustache, already bristling, became a forest of bayonets. He said in staccato tones:

"I had considered invoking the assistance of the police in the matter of the insupportable English. I, too, have been insulted, but grossly insulted, twice. The vessel which bears these scoundrels back to their vile country departs at six-fifteen. We will station ourselves by the gangway, Mademoiselle, and you will indicate to me the gentleman for whose sake you are in tears." The years between had gone, and he was back again, bloody but unbowed, before the Marne. With the ancient thunder of cannon in his ears and the fire of battle in his heart, he echoed the immortal exhortation of his greatest commander:

"Ils ne passeront pas."

CHAPTER NINETEEN

So absorbed was Luke Grenfell in the prose of André Gide that a considerable period of time elapsed before he noticed the absence of Shorty. He frowned and looked around the bookshop. There was no sign of the built-up shoulders or the ghastly tie. So much the better. But they would surely meet again, alas, at the ghoulish repast to be provided at five o'clock by Mr. Collins. Luke shuddered and went on reading. After a few minutes he made his way to the bookseller and enquired the price of André Gide. He bought the book, slipped it into his pocket and strolled towards the door. The bookseller, an old man, called softly:

"Excuse, please, Sir."

"Yes."

"Your friend, he has also taken a book, your friend who is gone away. He did not give me the money for the book."

"I'm most awfully sorry. How extraordinary!" Luke took off his spectacles, polished them and put them on again. "Er—how much was it?"

"A hundred and twenty francs."

Luke gave him the money at once. He said slowly and carefully, defending Shorty against his better judgment:

"You realise that this was clearly an oversight on my friend's part. He had no intention of not paying for the book. He is not a thief. He was merely absent-minded. You understand that?"

"Oh yes, I understand." He slid off his stool, and came over and stood beside Luke.

"Pay attention, Sir. Your friend and you arrive together. You, Monsieur, take up the André Gide. I say to myself, 'Ah-ha! Le English 'igh-brow.' I observe carefully how you touch the book with your hands, and again I say to myself, 'This one is a true lover of books.' I am content, even if you buy nothing. But your friend, he is not a 'igh-brow. On the contrary. He picks up a book, a *bêtise,* a nonsense. Your friend has no respect for the book, but only for the cover of the book."

There was something curiously deliberate about this

leisurely recital, and Luke had the sense that the bookseller somewhat fancied himself as a raconteur. He said with a shade of impatience:

"You have been paid for the book, and I have apologised for my friend's forgetfulness."

"It is worth your while to listen to me, Monsieur; please have patience. Your friend comes to you and demands that you explain, translate for him, the name of this foolish book. Yes?"

"Yes. But I fail to see——"

"You, Sir, translate the name. You talk for a moment with your friend. You smile. You are 'appy to return to André Gide. But your friend is not 'appy. Oh no." The bookseller stooped to approximately Shorty's height, and into his face came that same hunted look that Shorty had worn. His mimicry was superb. "Your friend look for a long time at the cover of this book—like this. But he does not see the cover. He sees something else. He is far from 'appy. You have seen a rabbit with one foot in a trap, when the man, the hunting-man, approaches with his big dog? The rabbit pulls this way, that way. But he must wait for the hand of the man or the teeth of the dog."

"Well?"

"That is how your friend look, like this rabbit. But he is not like the rabbit because he can escape." The bookseller straightened his back. "So that is what your friend does. 'E escapes, Monsieur. I would counsel you to look, to search, for your friend."

"Where did he go?" said Luke sharply.

"That I do not know for certain. I saw him consult in urgency with a policeman, and it is possible that I make a mistake." He shrugged. "But I do not think that I make a mistake."

"What do you think?"

The bookseller picked up a second copy of *Pour l'Amour d'un Légionnaire* and held it out.

"I think that your friend is guided by the cover of this foolish book. I think that he seeks to escape"—his voice sank—"to Sidi-bel-Abbès."

"But where the hell is Sidi-bel-Abbès?"

"It is a town in Algeria. It is the depot of the *Légion Etrangère.*"

"Good God!"

Luke stared at him.

The bookseller said reflectively:

"The hand of the man is more kind than are the teeth of the dog. If you wish to save your friend, it is possible that you are not too late. I would counsel you to go at once to the *Gendarmerie Nationale*. There I am sure you will find him. . . ."

The *Tricolor* hanging limp in the afternoon sun, a cobbled courtyard with a railed balcony on the first floor, a balcony with boxes of flowers, splashes of scarlet and purple and orange against the rusted rails; two somnolent policemen studying the results of yesterday's bicycle races, their boots on the counter of the enquiry office, a seemingly interminable wait, and then a summons to enter an inner room.

An enormous man in a blue uniform sprawled at a wooden table. His face was pallid and his eyes as expressionless as oysters. His tunic was unbuttoned and Luke Grenfell saw two, no three, rows of medal ribbons. The charred remnant of a *Gauloise* cigarette was stuck to his pendulous lower lip. He indicated a bentwood chair with an almost imperceptible jerk of a pudgy finger. The cigarette wobbled as he spoke.

"English?"

"Yes." Luke sat down nervously. "Good afternoon, Sir. I'm sorry to bother you but——"

"Your passport, please."

"My passport? Yes, of course."

The pudgy hand was extended. Luke gave him the passport. The expressionless eyes appeared not to see it, the pudgy hand returned it. The cigarette danced on the pendulous lip.

"You wish what?"

Luke leaned forward.

"Well, Sir, in a way it's not my business at all, but I gather that a man I know may have been here to see you this afternoon. He's a short chap, and he came over for the day on the boat from London this morning . . . with The Hand and Flower Darts Club. Everybody calls him Shorty, and I'm afraid I don't know his other name. I think he's pretty fed-up with life in general, and he may have come here with some crazy idea of joining the Foreign Legion. I wonder, Sir, if you'd let me sort of talk to him if he's still here—and if it's not too late. . . ."

That same expressionless stare, the pudgy, motionless hands, the dead cigarette; a dusty railway time-table pinned on the wall, a calendar for January 1944, printed in German; the eyes like oysters that had been opened a long time ago. Poor Shorty. Poor devil. . . .

"He is your friend—and you do not know his name."

"No. I don't know his name. We all call him 'Shorty'."

What unimagined hell had Shorty endured that he should seek refuge in this terrible place. The bookseller was right. Better the hand of the man than the teeth of the dog. He said slowly and with great sincerity:

"In a way, Sir, I feel that I'm to blame."

"Why?"

"I've never got on with him till this afternoon. We've been at daggers drawn for months. I ought to have seen what was going on a long time ago, and done something about it. But I didn't. It's largely my fault, Sir."

"Many of us are blind."

If only he'd blink or do something, even for a split second, to hood that lack-lustre stare. And somewhere, in this ghastly building, Shorty was sitting alone, on his way to God knows what new loneliness.

"Could I see him, Sir, if it's not too late . . . ?"

"It is not too late, Mr. Grenfell."

So the eyes had seen the passport. Luke said with a sigh:

"Well, thank the Lord for that."

The pudgy, seemingly motionless fingers must have moved, for a bell whirred in the outer room and the door opened. Without taking his eyes off Luke's face, the man's lower lip set the dead cigarette briefly dancing.

"*Amenez le petit.*"

"*Bien, mon Commandant.*"

Steps in the passage, a distant door opening and shutting, more steps, Shorty. Shorty with a strained face, Shorty's suit with the built-up shoulders, Shorty's mouth agape and angry now at the sight of Mr. Bloody Grenfell, the man from whom he had run away.

"You know this . . . this gentleman?"

"I know him. That's Mr. Grenfell . . . Sir."

The word 'sir' came with difficulty to Shorty's lips. It was the by-product of fear, fear of the man, the place, the future.

"Your friend wishes to talk to you."

Shorty shuffled his feet. He said obstinately:

"He's no friend of mine, and I got nothing to say to him nor nobody else. I made my mind up." His mouth tightened. "So you can sugar off, Lukey-boy, and leave me alone." He flung round to the impassive man in the blue uniform with the unbuttoned tunic. "Why did you let him come in here? I didn't ask him to come, did I, and, anyway, I joined the Foreign Legion, ain't I?"

There was silence. The oyster eyes flicked their gaze from Shorty to Luke Grenfell, flicked back to Shorty, perceived everything there was to see. As if by a miracle, the pallid face was transfigured by a smile that was warm with human understanding. The vast bulk rose, the pudgy fingers buttoned a straining tunic with its three—yes, three—rows of medal ribbons, were laid on Shorty's shoulders.

"Go with your friend, little one."

"But I've joined the Foreign Legion," said Shorty fiercely.

"True." A glimmer of laughter illuminated the oyster eyes, was instantly suppressed. "But you can be—what is the word? —honourably discharged. I too have served with the Legion. So we are already more than comrades, you and I. We are brothers, and until we die, we can say with pride that we have been legionnaires. I return you your passport. Take it. I salute you. Now go with your friend."

"Did I join the Foreign Legion or did I not?"

"You did."

"Right. Now that I'm in, I want to stay in—and I don't want Mr. Grenfell here chasing me round like a bloody nursemaid."

The officer lowered himself into his chair. He said with great patience:

"Listen to me, little one. The train for Lille does not leave until a quarter to six and, if you insist, it is my duty to give you a warrant. You would spend some days in the barracks at Lille. They are not very comfortable, and you would be very glad to go on to a new place, to the baracks of Saint Vincent at Marseille. From the barracks of Saint Vincent, you would consider the barracks at Lille to have been a de-luxe hotel. You would be very glad to leave Marseille, and to go on once more, to Sidi-bel-Abbès. Once in Sidi-bel-Abbès you would look back on Saint Vincent and know that you had been in paradise." He smiled. "The Legion is like that. The next station is always worse than the last. I know—because I, like you, have been a legionnaire. Accept your honourable discharge and go now with your friend. I am sure that he is your friend."

Shorty stiffened.

"It's no good trying to put the wind-up me. My mind's made up."

"Enough. I command you to go."

"I'll go—but I'll be back. No one's going to talk me out of it."

"We hear what you say. Now I would like to take my siesta."

There was a tense silence. Luke Grenfell broke it.

"Come on you b.f.," he said to Shorty. "Dammit, you owe me a hundred and twenty francs for the book you pinched." He turned to the officer. "Thank you most awfully, Sir. May I . . . er . . . offer you a cigarette?"

"No, thank you, Mr. Grenfell. I have one." With a flourish he set fire to the black stub.

They stood side by side leaning over the ramparts, looking over the roofs of Boulogne. It was a long time before Shorty spoke. He said angrily:

"I didn't mean to pinch that book. I forgot I had it in my hand. I may be a lot of things, but I'm not a thief."

"I know you're not."

"I'd like to give you the money for it. I'm not a thief."

"Nobody ever thought you were a thief."

Shorty laughed with bitter sarcasm.

"Nobody—except you and the C.I.D. How much did the bloody book cost?"

"Hundred and twenty francs."

"Fine. Here it is. And now, provided nursey has no objection, I'll be getting back." He went on trying deliberately to wound, "You got what you came for."

He turned and began to walk away. Luke did not move. So immobile was he that he might have been a carved figure looking for ever with sightless eyes of stone from the ramparts of the city. He heard Shorty's quick steps become slower, heard them hesitate and drag and stop. He knew that Shorty had turned round and was looking at him with resentment, and that the slightest move on his part would be the signal for those hideous pointed shoes to take up their march once more. He waited. Far below, a fishing-boat with a brown sail tacked into harbour from the open sea, crawled with an ever-diminishing bow-wave to her mooring. Suddenly, Shorty's shoes crunched on the gravel beside him. Shorty's voice spoke at his side, veined with an emotion which he himself did not understand.

"Mr. Grenfell."

"Yes, Shorty?"

"I'm sorry I said that—about you only coming for the money."

"That's all right."

"I know you was only trying to do your best, but it's no good. I wouldn't like to go away with you thinking I thought you only wanted your hundred and twenty francs. That's all." He paused. "Damn your eyes. I'm not one to apologise. And now sugar off."

The fishermen were alongside the quay and the brown sail was flapping down off the mast. Luke said meditatively, gazing over the harbour:

"What's the trouble, Shorty?"

"Trouble? I'm in no trouble. Not now, anyway. I just want to get away."

"Away from what?"

"You wouldn't understand."

"I could try. I hope you'll give me a chance to try."

"I'd be wasting my bloody time."

"Well . . . waste it. It's the last chance you'll get."

"How tall are you?"

"Five foot ten."

"You look bigger. If you was to stand up straight you'd be six feet—or a bit more. And now look me over," he said with bitterness. "It won't take you long. I'm Shorty, I am. Shorty the little runt, knee-high to a duck, Shorty the coppers' half-holiday, four foot eleven in his high-heel shoes, and every inch of it good for a laugh. But I *could* be somebody different, and neither you nor no one else is going to stop me."

"Going to Sidi-bel-Abbès won't increase your height."

"I never said it would. But it'll increase *me*."

"I don't understand."

"I told you I'd be wasting my bloody time, talking to you."

"Please go on."

"All right. You've asked for it. You'll get it." He looked over the harbour, but he saw nothing of the roofs or the ruins or the masts of ships. He peered instead into the future and, for the first time in his life, he was happy at what he saw. He went on, speaking more slowly now, delighting in the image of what was to come:

"I join the Foreign Legion. I serve my time—and even if it's tough, I can take it. Well, when I've served my time, I come out. I come back to England. O.K. Well, one night, I stroll into the old Hand and Flower. Mrs. Collins and the boys see me come in. What do they say? 'Well, well, there's Shorty! Where you dropped from, Shorty?' What do I say? 'Africa, actually. Sahara, as a matter of fact—and less of the Shorty, *if* you please. Maybe one or two of you gentlemen seen "Beau Geste". Well, that's me. I been in the Foreign Legion, see. And now, laugh that one off.' "

Luke saw it all.

"There's few," said Shorty, "big or small, as can say that."

What was Shorty prepared to endure in return for this far-distant, imagined moment of triumph? Loneliness, discipline so rigid as to be sadistic, the jeers not of his compatriots but of strangers from whom he would be separated by the gulf of an unknown language, years of sweat and toil, with the brief, nightly solace of oblivion. Aware, now, that he was fighting a losing battle, Luke said without conviction:

"But . . . but what about your parents?"

"Parents!" Shorty spat derisively. "Don't be funny, Chum. I was born in Holloway Jail, and my Mum died on the parish this long time. I never seen my dad and my mum only seen him once." Shorty sniffed. "Once too often that was—for that's where I came in. But I got a half-sister, a nice, well-spoken young lady, name of Beryl. I told you about her. Her dad isn't my dad. He's her real dad." He paused and added succinctly, "Churched."

"But surely you've got a girl-friend . . . or somebody."

"Girl-friend! Me! The only place I could find a girl-friend would be in the freak pit of a bloody circus." He drew himself up to his meagre height and said with great sarcasm, "Well, Mr. Grenfell Sir, any more questions?"

"No, Shorty. No more questions. But there is one favour I want to ask of you."

"*You* asking *me* favours? Don't make me laugh."

"You can laugh if you like, but I still want to ask you a favour. Wherever you get to, and I don't know what lies before you, write and tell me where and how you are."

"I'm no good at writing. Never could spell."

"Well . . . try."

Shorty shifted his feet. "O.K. I'll try."

"Promise."

"Aw, nuts. If I say I will, I will."

"Fair enough. You'll always find me care of The Hand and Flower, Saint John's Wood, London. Please remember that, as a solid thing."

"I'll write. Although what good it'll do me, I don't know." He began to stammer. He had remembered the man with the oyster eyes, and what might lie beyond the gate through which he soon would pass filled him with fear. "Well, I'd b-b-better be getting b-b-back now. And, as I said before, I d-d-didn't mean what I said about your only coming for the m-m-money, s-s-straight up, I d-d-didn't. S-s-solong, and all the b-b-best."

"So long, Shorty."

His stammer fled. He said truculently:

"You won't call me 'Shorty' when I come home—from the Foreign Legion."

"I'll never call you 'Shorty' again. What's your real name? I've never known."

"My real name?" He grinned sheepishly. "Aw, skip it. Just call me 'Bill'. Bill will do."

"But is Bill your name?"

"No, it isn't. My name is Nelson Rodney Drake Frobisher Harris." His ghastly shoes did their little hornpipe on the gravel and he scowled. "Funny, isn't it? My dad was a sailor, see, like you. Well, all the b-b-best, Lukey-boy."

"All the best, Bill."

He turned to watch Shorty go. He walked with his arms swinging and his back erect, the travesty of a Guardsman, four foot eleven inches of determination and guts. He passed under the limp *Tricolor,* turned to the right. There was a silent roll of drums, and the noble music of a song surged in Luke Grenfell's memory. Looking at the gate through which Shorty had passed, he said aloud:

> "*Allons, enfants de la patrie,*
> *Le jour de gloire est arrivé. . .* "

CHAPTER TWENTY

Jim Carver walked down the steep street. He had little sense of direction at this moment, but he knew that he must eventually come to the harbour and that was where he wanted to be. He walked quickly, seeing nothing but his destination. From the moment when Marie-Josephe had held out her hand to him in the *Cimetière de l'Est* he had only wished to arrest the passage of time. Now the pendulum had swung violently—and the boat could not leave too soon.

His hurt mind refused to admit what he knew deep down to be the root and the reason for Marie-Josephe's sudden attack and equally sudden withdrawal, and he kept making excuses for himself, attributing her flight to any cause other than the true one. Had he—an Englishman—been too diffident with a Frenchwoman, or had he—a man—been too bold with a girl? He told himself that by the time the cliffs of Kent rose out of the sea he would be able to think more clearly and see with detachment why and at what point the golden thread had snapped. He lied to himself, for he knew now. His steps became slower. Ever since Marie-Josephe had spoken to him near to where George Holden lay, he had had a blinding sense of the inevitable. It had begun even before that. It had been with him last night—and the bells of Saint Saviour's had chimed the advent of this extraordinary day, lacing the dawn with the echo of a song he thought long ago to have forgotten. The song learned among the apple trees was no longer an echo. It had become real and remembered, and he had listened to it, sung by a living voice over the graves of the dead. Every step took him farther and farther away from the singer—and, in God's name, why? What sudden lunacy had prompted him to defend himself against the shock of hearing that Marie-Josephe was promised in marriage by claiming an engagement to which he was in no way bound? And there had been plenty of time over the day for him to have put things right. He'd never done it. He'd let Marie-Josephe go on believing what wasn't true.

He stopped. With a tremendous gush of love, he understood clearly how the mind of a clean and honourable girl had worked. Her bitterness had been a bitterness derived from simple honesty. Through a gap between two shattered houses he had a narrow glimpse of the harbour and of the blue levels of the sea. There lay journey's end. Behind him, if he had the grace and strength to go back, might be journey's beginning.

Again the pendulum swung and every minute became as precious as gold. Jim turned away from the road to the harbour, and began, slowly at first, to retrace his steps up the street that led to the Cathedral. His pace quickened from a walk to a march. Half-way up the hill he had to stop to breathe and to wipe the sweat from his forehead. He used the only handkerchief he had, and it was not his own. The sight of it was like the touch of a spur. Though the sun burned his face like a furnace, though his shirt was soaked and every muscle in his legs had its own separate ache, he strode on. He knew what he would say to Marie-Josephe if there were need for words between them. He would take her two hands in his and tell her the truth, then everything would be as it had been in *Clos d'Argent* and in the Cathedral. The future would take care of itself. His only purpose was to reach the steps, and to go to her and clasp her bare, sunburned fingers. The road canted steeply upwards, and he half-ran the last fifty yards and swung breathlessly round the corner.

The sound of his eager feet made a great clatter in the emptiness. The steps of the Cathedral, long-shadowed in the declining sun, the cobbles of the street, petrified ripples in a petrified sea, the blind, sunbaked houses, all these things were as still and as hot and as brooding as a Van Gogh.

Trevor Hilgrove glanced at his watch and yawned. For the last three-quarters of an hour he had been indulging in one of his favourite pastimes, that of watching the world go by. He sat under a striped umbrella outside one of the humbler cafés, not far from the Etoile, and contemplated the future with an equanimity amounting to smugness. Everything had gone remarkably well—and the incident with the old General in the black eyeglass had merely served to add a *sauce piquante* to an already stimulating adventure. His dart-board —original price thirty shillings—was now worth about five hundred pounds. He picked it up carefully and examined it with meticulous attention. Yes, the job had been well done, for the join was almost invisible to the naked eye. He knew, of course, that the observant gentlemen of Her Majesty's Customs and Excise studied the passengers as closely as they did their luggage, and that once their suspicions were aroused the game was up for the guilty. It was unlikely that, even allowing for their photographic memory for faces, they would isolate his features from those of The Hand and Flower Darts Club. Suppose they did, suppose they invited him courteously to enter the special examination room so that he could be searched and his belongings weighed, all would *still* be well. Trevor proposed to take no chances. Charley Brewer, with his blue serge suit, his bowler, his gym-shoes and his spread pig-ears collar, was the most transparently innocent of men. No Customs officers would give him more than a humorous glance. It was Charley, therefore, who would have the unwitting honour of transporting five-hundred-pounds' worth of gold watches through the Customs Hall of Folkestone. Nothing could be easier. He would stand Charley a few drinks on board ship, and then say something like, "Look, Charley, I've been carrying this blasted thing round all day. Time you took a turn. Fair's fair." Once past the hawk-eyed Waterguard and safely on the train to Victoria, he would relieve Charley of his burden and—yes, he would—he'd buy him a large whisky and soda.

Trevor looked at the passers-by with a pity that was veined with contempt. Simple *Boulonnais,* how purposeless were their wanderings. How hard they toiled for a pittance, a few thousand francs in the month to keep body, soul and family together, a few hundred to spend grudgingly in the cafés. One or two of them glanced at his dart-board, symbol of the English day-tripper, and smiled with knowing tolerance. Trevor smiled back. Why not? He could afford to smile.

He supposed that it was already time to get back to the Etoile. Funny that Jim Carver never turned up. He was the only mysterious one of the party, and therefore the only one of interest to Trevor Hilgrove. He'd gone off alone as soon as the boat docked, and nobody seemed to have any idea where he'd gone, except that ass Luke Grenfell. That was another queer thing, come to think of it. People were apt to confide in Luke Grenfell, in spite of his horn-rimmed spectacles and his slightly donnish air. Could it be that he possessed some quality, some—he frowned—some integrity that was not apparent to one who lived by his wits? Not that it mattered a damn either way. Suddenly he started. There, surely, was Jim Carver—and looking like the wrath of God! He stood up, almost tripping over his dart-board, and waved.

"Jim."

Jim turned instantly, eagerly. When he saw Trevor, the interest in his face died. Trevor called cheerfully:

"Hullo, Jim. Come and have a drink."

Jim hesitated. Then slowly and with an air of weariness, he threaded his way through the tables and sat down. The observant Trevor noticed that he deliberately chose a seat that commanded the widest view of the street, and that his grey eyes glanced swiftly at and away from every woman that passed. He said meaningly:

"Looking for someone, Jim?"

"No. Not really. Well, I am, in a way. Sorry I couldn't turn up. I had to go and see some . . . some friends, and they kept me longer than I thought."

"Have a drink, Jim."

At last Jim Carver turned and looked at him directly. His lean face was strained and set, and Trevor was at once aware that something had gone pretty badly astray. Jim squared his shoulders.

"Yes," he said, "I will. I've just realised that I've a raging thirst. We might even split a bottle."

"Damn good idea. Drown our sorrows in drink. Old Collins is expecting us all in the Etoile at five, and it's after that now, so we mustn't be too long." He said carelessly, "Shall we drink it inside where it's cool?"

"No. I'd rather we stayed here, if you don't mind."

"Just as you like. I only thought we might get out of the sun."

"No. Not out of the sun."

Trevor called the waiter, and after a little friendly wrangling, ordered a bottle of white Bordeaux. With a nice sense of the fitness of things, he chose a dry *Entre Deux Mers*. The bottle was misted and cold to the touch and the wine redolent of the scent of flowers. He poured out two glasses and raised his with a grin.

"'Always hold a bottle by the neck and a woman by the waist', as my grandfather used to say."

It wasn't true. He hadn't got a grandfather—at least not

one whose maxims were worth quoting. But his alleged descent from a robust old wine-bibber with a few imaginary acres of rough shooting in an unspecified part of the West Country, went very well with his old school tie. Trevor had several of these gambits, all designed to increase his social status. He frequently produced an equally imaginary old nurse, who was quite a character in her own way and whose comments on life below stairs were as diverting as they were pungent. In strictly non-military society, he was apt to quote the witticisms of 'one of my sergeants', among soldiers the same witticisms came from 'one of my snotties'. He had one remark that always went with a swing in almost any society. It was 'lovely scentin' morning'. Now he groped among a considerable selection to find the most appropriate toast and decided on the *débonnaire,* the dashing.

"Well," he said gaily, "here's to women and gunpowder—God bless 'em both."

"What?"

"I said 'women and gunpowder'. It's a sort of joke."

"Oh, I see. Well, all the best."

"All the best," said Trevor humbly.

That hadn't gone with a swing. Obviously the timing was wrong.

"Had a good day, Jim?"

He didn't want to speak to Hilgrove about his day. There was only one person he felt he could talk to with any freedom. Well—there were two, actually, but one of them was dead.

"Yes. I've . . . I've had quite a good day. How did you get on?"

"We all had lunch together, followed by a pretty boring speech from old Collins. Then we separated and went off on our own. As a matter of fact, I went to see—a sick friend, and then afterwards I got involved in a slight *fracas* with an old b.f. in a black eyeglass." Trevor laughed. "The old boy was so livid that he presented me with his card. Here it is." He read it aloud, smiling, "'*Général Felix de la Chanterelle, Grand Officer of the Legion of Honour*', and all that sort of tripe."

"You don't get the Legion of Honour for nothing. At least, not often. What happened?"

"We had a bit of a set-to, that's all. When he gave me his card, he asked me for mine, so I fished him out one I'd been given by the tout at the harbour this morning. Damn funny. I'd like to have seen his face when he read it."

"But you didn't wait?"

"No fear. I'm not looking for trouble. I gave him the tout's card and beat it, so if you happen to spot a military-looking gent in white buckskin shoes, wearing a black eyeglass and carrying a stick, take my advice and keep out of his way. I don't think he likes the English—much."

"It's a pity," said Jim. "That sort of thing does no good."

"Oh, rot," said Trevor easily. "All's well that ends well." He drained his glass. There was a little wine left in the bottle. "That's your share, Jim. Drink it up and we'll get along to the Etoile and meet the others."

"I'm not going to the Etoile. I'm staying here."

"But my dear chap——"

"I'm staying here . . . until the boat goes. Would you tell Mr. Collins that I'm quite all right and that I'll meet him on board."

Trevor stood up and counted out half the price of the wine in franc notes. He said in a friendly voice, inviting a confidence:

"There's my half. Anything up, Jim?"

"No, nothing at all. I'm fine—but I want to stay here . . . in case my friend, the person I know, happened to come by. Not that that's likely."

"If there's anything I can do, let me know. I speak the language a bit, and if there's anything, well you've only got to say the word."

"No. There's nothing anyone can do. Sorry. The best service you could do would be to leave me alone. Sorry. I'm not being rude, but that's how it is."

Trevor looked at him strangely. Whatever it was that had hit Jim Carver had hit him bloody hard. The parcel he'd been holding on to so carefully in the train and in the boat had gone, and Trevor wondered if it could have anything to do with that. He didn't suppose he'd ever find out. Jim wasn't the talking kind.

"O.K., Jim. See you on board."

"You will. Don't forget your precious dart-board."

'Precious'. Why had Jim used the word 'precious'? But he was scanning the street with that same intensity, hoping desperately that someone would appear, so that he could start up and go to whoever it was. The word, the *mot juste,* had been accidental, and was without significance. Odd to think of Jim Carver, of all people, being caught up in an emotional tangle, for that's what had clearly happened. He'd thought of Jim as the solemn, steady sort, one of 'the mere uncounted folk'. Showed how wrong one could be. He picked up the dart-board. It *was* heavy, damned heavy. Still, with the rollicking Charley Brewer carrying it, no one would bother to look at it twice—please God! He said lightly:

"Hope your friend turns up, Jim. So long."

"So long."

If only she would come. Surely among those who passed and repassed, he would catch a glimpse of her pale, proud face and dark hair. He would know her instantly by her walk alone, white high-heeled sandals stepping delicately, deliberately, a green silk dress, the medal of Our Lady, the sunburned fingers, bare now. Where could she have gone to? Back to *Clos d'Argent*? But then she couldn't start the car without him, so she must be somewhere near. Would it be better for him to walk the streets or to stay here? If she passed, she would pass by this place. If she went to her friend, Madame Loget, she would still have to tread this pavement. There was one place that she might have gone to and, if she had, then she would have gone from him for ever. She might have hidden that pale circle on her finger with Henri's ring once more and be with him now.

What a fool he'd been. It was no use his pretending to himself that he didn't know why she had gone, when he knew perfectly well. In his first blinding disappointment, he had wanted to blame her, to find excuses for himself by saying that she was impulsive and irresponsible. The opposite was the truth. It was she who had been consistent throughout, he who had failed to measure up to her honesty. When he had asked her about her ring, she had told him simply and at once that it had been given to her by her fiancé, by Henri Dubot. She had said, "And you, Jim? What about you?" and he had produced Cherry. He had not produced a woman of flesh and blood, but a defence mechanism. It would have been so easy, at any time of the day, to have said to her what was the truth, that Cherry and he had drifted into the sort of association that can so readily come to men who live alone in London; that it was an association without any passion or any real intimacy, and that he had no obligation whatsoever to pursue it to its end, as foreseen by Miss Mitchell. But he hadn't done that. He had let Cherry sit with them at lunch, he had taken her round *Clos d'Argent* at Marie-Josephe's side. She had ridden in the car with them, and she, too, had walked up the aisle of Notre Dame de Boulogne, to kneel and to pray, invisible as she was terrible, dividing them for ever. And now—what? And now nothing. Marie-Josephe had gone, all he had left was a square of sweat-soaked linen. It wasn't much.

One thing was sure. He had finished with London. He had done well, and he knew that if he stayed he would do even better. But there was no point in doing well in a place where you didn't want to be, in a place full of Cherry Mitchells, decent, friendly girls, who trapped you into a soft, shared mesh of easy living, when you didn't want to live easily. You wanted to live a muscular life, working the land, breaking the stubborn soil. There was that strip of field, over beyond the Windrush, choked with nettles and brambles and bracken it was, but it could be a lovely bit of grass after a bit, if it was cleared and ploughed and sowed and harrowed. After a year or so you could run three or four heifers on it. . . .

"Hullo, Jim."

Luke Grenfell sat down in the chair that Trevor Hilgrove had left. He lit a *Gauloise* in silence. The waiter came up and stood expectantly. Luke took up the empty bottle and looked at the label.

"Care to split another bottle of this, Jim?"

"Yes. I'd like to. I'm damn thirsty."

"Me, too."

He ordered the wine and stretched his long legs.

"Hilgrove told me you were here, so I thought I'd come along."

"I'm glad you came."

The two men sat in silence while the wine was brought and poured out. Women and girls passed in flowered frocks, in black, in white, in red. But there was no sign of a green silk dress and high-heeled sandals, no sign at all.

"Boat goes in about forty minutes, Jim."

"I know."

"Shorty's not coming back with us."

"Why not?"

"He's joined the Foreign Legion. It's easy to do, at least the mechanics are easy. You just go to the Gendarmerie Nationale and sign on. It's when you're in that it isn't easy. But Shorty's done it. I've never liked Shorty much until today. But he's full of guts, poor little devil."

"But can anybody just go and join the Foreign Legion?"

"Yes. Anybody can. I believe that they make private enquiries about you, and if you're wanted by the police they turf you out again. But anybody can start—and Shorty has."

"Bit of a shock for Mr. Collins, isn't it?"

"Shock!" Luke Grenfell laughed. "Collins is incapable of shock any more. Charley Brewer turned up at the Etoile with old Collins in tow and, believe it or not, the Licensee of The Hand and Flower had the perfect imprint in lipstick of some woman's mouth all over his cheek. Charley had met him somewhere, and hadn't told him that it was there. I've never seen anyone in my life look more like a pricked balloon than Collins, and of course Charley's having the time of his life. Full of Benedictine, champagne and moral indignation."

"You've had quite a day, haven't you?"

"Yes—and that's not all. A couple of chaps in the Etoile took Hilgrove's dart-board when he wasn't looking and hung it up on the wall and started shying darts at it. My God, you'd think someone had let off a 36 hand-grenade when Hilgrove saw them. He kicked up a fearful shindy about it. Dammit, that's what a dart-board's for. Now he's nursing the thing like a newborn baby. Comic chap, Hilgrove. I don't like him much."

Jim Carver only half listened. Now there were only a bare thirty minutes left to him. He supposed, wearily, that he should be interested in what had happened to his friends, but he couldn't be when his mind was drenched with the image of Marie-Josephe, and when his eyes only sought for one more glimpse of a green frock and a proud, defiant face.

"Did you find your friend, George Holden?"

"Oh yes. I found George all right." He went on looking with hope that ebbed with every passing minute. "Yes, I found him. Do you remember, in the train this morning, that I asked you if you had ever heard of a song called 'Savez-vous planter les choux'?"

"I remember very well. I told you that it was an old song, as old as France."

"Well, I found the . . . the girl who taught it to me."

"Ah!"

"You can say 'ah' as much as you like. I suppose you think I've just been hanging round with a woman all day. I suppose you think that I'm like Charley Brewer. Well, you're bloody well wrong. It's not like that."

"I have never thought any such thing. Tell me, Jim—if you want to."

"I told you coming over on the boat about George Holden, and how we'd planned, when the war was over, to go into a sort of partnership to work the land. Well, all that went to hell when George was killed and I got a job in London. This girl"—he swallowed—"her name is Marie-Josephe, by the way, this girl runs a farm with arable and pasture and stock. It's a long way back there, over beyond the Cathedral, and she's got the feel of it in her finger-tips. With her I began to see the whole thing working again. George and I were going in for clearing first and sowing grass, and then, gradually, we were going to upgrade the Shorthorns, breeding to blood-lines. Then we had what I suppose you'd call a damn silly scheme. I thought, we both thought, that one day the whole world might be a hungry place, and we'd worked out an idea to keep country children interested in the land and stop that drift to the pin-table saloons and the petrol stations. But the whole thing would work with Marie-Josephe. I know damn well it would."

"How old is your Marie-Josephe?"

"About twenty-one or twenty-two, I suppose. I don't know. She was only a little girl when she taught me the song, years ago, in the war."

"Is she pretty, Jim?"

Jim said solemnly, "She's the most beautiful girl I've ever seen in my life."

Luke Grenfell lit another *Gauloise*. He said gently:

"And you say you saw this young and beautiful girl in the role of . . . of female agricultural labourer?"

"No, I didn't."

"Then how did you see her?"

"I saw her as the person I've been waiting for always."

"Did you tell her so?"

"No. I . . . I hadn't the right to tell her anything of how I felt about her until just before we separated. Then it was too late."

"I don't think it's ever too late, Jim." He stood up. He said with affection, "Some day, when I meet your Marie-Josephe, I'll tell her what an ass she was to let you go, even for a little while."

"But you won't ever see her. I tell you, she's gone. God knows where she is—and the boat goes in twenty minutes."

"Listen to me, Jim. Shorty knew what he wanted, and he's cutting his way through to it with a sword. You've got a ploughshare in your hand. Don't be a fool for the rest of your life. See you soon."

"You will."

The pavements were less crowded now, as the men and women of Boulogne began to make their way to their homes. A cool breath of wind lifted the tablecloth and set the bay trees rustling dryly. From the belfries of the town the chiming of the hour was like a flight of pigeons across the evening sky. Jim Carver drew a deep breath and shivered. The sweat had dried on his body, and he felt cold, cold and stiff and infinitely tired.

He didn't even bother to look for Marie-Josephe any more, so certain was he that the day had run its course. Slowly and with great sadness he took the road to the harbour.

CHAPTER TWENTY-ONE

Général de la Chanterelle and Marie-Josephe walked the ramparts of Boulogne side by side.

"By a strange coincidence," said the General icily, "I happened to be reading Rousseau's *Emile* only last night. Permit me, Mademoiselle, to quote you a passage. *'Great eaters of meat are in general more cruel and ferocious than other men. The cruelty of the English is known.'* "

"That can hardly be true today," said Marie-Josephe sadly, "for on all sides one hears that the English at home have to sustain themselves on one mouthful a week. It is said that their post-war knowledge of the French language may be concentrated into two words—*'Chateaubriand garni.'* "

"Exactly, Mademoiselle. They only come to France to satisfy their gluttony, to eat, to drink and pillage."

"Jim Carver didn't come for any of these things, *Monsieur le Général.*"

"Then for what purpose did he come?"

"He came to visit the grave of his friend, who was killed while a soldier in the British Army."

The General softened.

"I do not claim that all the English are wild beasts. I myself have had experience of the British Army, and I confess that I found gentlemen amongst them, gentlemen and brave men. The English at war are supportable. The English at peace are insupportable. Today, Mademoiselle, we are at peace."

"It is a strange peace in which we live today, *Monsieur le Général*. Often at night when the wind is in the north-east, have you not heard the sound of the guns of English ships as they prepare, once again, to defend their island? It will be a sad affair for France, I think, when the English can no longer fire their guns for their country and for ours."

"Mademoiselle, I do not wish to discuss the political uncertainties of the world with one who is little more than a child. On two separate occasions, within thirty minutes of each other, I have been insulted by the English. Let that pass. I am a man and I can recompense myself in my own manner.

But you, you are a woman and I demand that you indicate the heartless villain who has brought tears to your pretty eyes. He will discover that not even a grand English milord can lightly cause distress to a Frenchwoman. *On verra.*"

"*Monsieur le Général,* you force me to relate the circumstances whereby you discovered me in tears. May we not seat ourselves for a moment? It is more than half an hour that we walk these ramparts as if they were a barrack square, and I . . . I am very tired."

"My dear child." The General was instantly contrite. He led her to a seat and removed his panama hat. Folding his hands on his silver-topped stick, he glanced at his watch and gazed over the roofs and the chimneys in the direction of the harbour. "We have ten minutes before it is necessary to descend, and you may be assured that I shall respect your confidence."

"Of that I am certain. Mine is not a long but a simple story, and when I have told it to you, you will understand why I, too, *Monsieur le Général,* find it difficult to believe that the English soldiers are other than gentlemen and brave men."

"Mademoiselle, I am reluctantly prepared to be convinced."

"When the British came to France in 1944, a squadron, a troop of tanks, came to rest for a space in the orchard of my father. They had been in many battles, and they were going on to many more battles. They were English Lancers. I was only a little girl, but these soldiers were very welcome to us. One of them was . . . was Sergeant Jim Carver. He was one who was gentle and strong and kind, and to me he gave the badge from his beret, the two lances with the crown of the English king. He also assisted me to make butter in the dairy, and I taught him a song and he taught me English words. When he went away I was sad, for a very long time. I never thought to see this man again. Today, this morning, we met in the *Cimetière de l'Est,* and it was as if he had never gone away. I had become affianced to Henri Dubot and he, Jim, has also engaged himself to marry an English lady." She paused. She said defiantly, "I am no longer affianced to Henri Dubot. That affair is at an end for ever."

"Ha! And the Englishman, what about him?"

"That, *Monsieur le Général,* is a question to which I do not know the answer. So overjoyed was I during the hours of the day that I permitted him to see that . . . that it was with me as if he had never gone away. I think I was a great idiot. Then, at last, when he said that he wished to take me into his arms, I considered the lady he should marry and . . . and to stop myself from becoming an even greater idiot, I was very rude to him. I said things, terrible things, that would make him go away."

"And he went?"

"Yes. He went. His face became set with eyes of stone, and he only said 'Good-bye, Marie-Josephe', and all of a moment he was gone." She turned and said passionately, "So you see that it is all without hope. Surely if it were possible for him to think of me, he would at that moment have taken me in his arms and commanded me to hold my tongue? It was all that was necessary."

"You will find the reason, my unhappy one, in the works of Voltaire. 'The gloomy Englishman, even in his loves, always wants to reason.' " He stood up. "Come, Child, we will go together to the point of departure. I will obtain satisfaction for the insults to which I have been subjected, and you, you will see if your Englishman is still of the same mind."

"But I never wish to see him again. Never. And more than that, I do not wish him to see me."

"Doubtless," said the General dryly, "you are now considering which order of nuns you will enter."

"But yes. How did you know?"

"I am not only a father, Mademoiselle, but a grandfather. Which of these two things do you wish the most? Not to see, or not to be seen?"

"Both."

"In that case," said the General briskly, "all I can do is to assist you to start the motor of your car and to bid you good evening. I, Mademoiselle, have serious matters to attend to."

Although the General was standing impatiently by her, Marie-Josephe made no move. So high as to be almost invisible, a lark was singing over the dome of the Cathedral, and she was reminded sharply and with sadness of how she and Jim had listened together to that song. A melodious clamour of bells drowned the singing of the lark, but it rose again, thin and insistent. She traced a pattern in the warm dust with the toe of her sandal.

"Perhaps, *Monsieur le Général,* it would be better if I were to accompany you. Remember another of the sayings of Voltaire, *'The English people are people who always defend themselves.'* These savages might do you an injury." She jumped to her feet. "It will be necessary for us to hurry, for the boat departs at a quarter-past six. Possibly you will be kind enough to turn the handle of my car. I know a short way to the quay and, once there, I can conceal myself, neither seeing nor being seen."

The Hand and Flower Darts Club was coming home. Led by Charley Brewer playing 'Colonel Bogey' on his mouth-organ and with the haggard Mr. Collins bringing up the rear, the tiny band of pilgrims trudged slowly along the cobbled quay towards the impatient ship. Mr. Collins walked with downcast head, his left cheek burning more fiercely from the memory of what had been imprinted upon it than from the harsh soap with which he had expunged the symbol of his shame. For the hundredth time since that fatal moment when the bead curtains had parted to admit Charley, Mr. Collins remembered with sick despair the innocent but utterly damning sequence of events that had led to his downfall. All he'd wanted to do was to listen for a minute to the gramophone—for it was to the tune of 'Baby Doll' that he had courted Emma nigh on thirty-four years ago. He used to call her his 'little bit o' fluff' in those days, just like the officers did, and even after they were married they still used to call it 'our tune'. But from the moment he'd walked in to listen he had become as clay in the hands of the harpy inside, and he had watched, as if at a distance and with a fearful fascination, the person of the licensee of The Hand and Flower being subjected to one indignity after another. She had twirled his quiff, unlaced his boots, bitten his ear, stolen his medal for playing outside-left for the Palmers Green Rovers, charged him over two pounds for a bottle of champagne that he hadn't even ordered, and, grossest insult of all—she had purloined unto herself the words of 'Baby Doll', words sacred to Mrs. Collins. Every protestation had been turned into an alleged advance, every attempt at flight rendered merely laughable because of the limpet-like manner in which she had attached herself to the lap of his best trousers.

His humiliation was complete. Not only had he himself courted disaster, but those for whom he was responsible had run into trouble, each in his own way. Jim Carver—well, to be honest he didn't know about Jim—but his own experience, coupled with that of the team, could only lead him to suppose that Jim, too, had met his moral Waterloo. And he a nice, steady chap, practically engaged to Cherry Mitchell if all he heard was right, not that he ever gave an ear to talk, not a man in his position.

His position! What was his position now? Mr. Collins groaned. And he hadn't even got a pair of nylons, size ten and a half, and a nice beige . . .

Shorty! Shorty had gone off and joined the Foreign Legion. Nice that would be when Shorty's mum—if Shorty had a mum—came round to The Hand and Flower and started to create. 'Pardon me, Mr. Collins, but I'd be most interested to hear the whereabouts of my boy, if you don't mind. . . ."

Perhaps the biggest disappointment of all had been Mr. Hilgrove. Only last night Emma had turned to him and said in her very own words, "I'm ever so glad Mr. Hilgrove's going, too, Fred. Adds a bit of tone, somehow; he's quite the gentleman, Mr. Hilgrove is." And what had happened? Mr. Hilgrove had gone off on his own after middle-day dinner and had only turned up again at the end, for his tea at the Eatoyle. Even then he'd been quite the gentleman—until a couple of strangers had picked up his dart-board when he wasn't looking, and hung it up on the wall and started to play. You'd think the blasted thing was made of gold the way he went on, cursing and swearing and creating. Really, Mr. Collins would have called the police—if he hadn't been too busy ordering a bottle of champagne for Charley and praying that this unwonted generosity would seal the lips of the Captain of The Hand and Flower Darts Club for ever. Up to now, Charley hadn't spoken. But what he *had* done was to let Mr. Collins appear before the others with the mark of the beast on his left cheek; he'd said to Mr. Collins casually, meaningly, "I could do with a bottle of the same stuff you was a-drinking of last time we met, Mr. C.," and then, when the bottle had been paid for, he'd raised his glass and said:

"Well, here's to them as keep themselves to themselves."

The only gentleman who'd behaved himself from start to

finish as a gentleman was Mr. Grenfell. Him and Mr. Hetherington, Mr. Thomson, Mr. Johnson and Mr. Pratt.

"Oh God."

If only he'd got a pair of nylons, size ten and a half, and a nice beige. . . .

Trevor Hilgrove walked the cobbled quay. Though he found it more than distasteful to be forced to follow the martial music of one who was half-seas over, if wholly triumphant, he marched with a good grace. A sinner on what he liked to consider the grand scale, Trevor had little sympathy with those who committed mere peccadilloes. What did it matter if Charley had come upon Collins in *flagrante delicto*? Though it was a situation that would give the greatest satisfaction to the customers of The Hand and Flower for months to come, it interested Trevor not at all. His sole preoccupation was to ingratiate himself still more closely with Charley, so that, when the time came and the vessel was in sight of Folkestone, he would produce his well-rehearsed phrase. How did it go?

"Look, Charley, I've been carrying this blasted thing round all day. Time you took a turn. After all, fair's fair."

And things had damn nearly gone wrong, damn nearly. When he had seen those chaps shying darts at five hundred quids' worth of dart-board, his temper—always touchy—had burst like a bomb and there had been a brief but ugly scene. He had recovered his equanimity with an effort, and the incident—forgotten in Mr. Collins's discomfiture—had passed off.

Trevor Hilgrove had a taste for the grotesque. It pleased him mightily and added zest to his day that he should march behind a tipsy coalman playing 'Colonel Bogey', while across his back he carried the symbol of genial democracy, literally lined with gold.

"Oh, my God," said the Purser to the Chief Steward, "here they come."

"Pretty to watch, Cyril. Pretty to watch."

They had shown their passports, had them stamped, been given their boarding cards, denied hotly that they were taking any francs out of France, said that they had nothing to declare, nothing at all. Obligingly, Trevor had turned round so that the lady examiner might scrawl her hieroglyphics in chalk on his dart-board. The formalities of leaving France were over, and it was only left to the remaining members of The Hand and Flower Darts Club to cross the cobbles, ascend the gangway and make their way to the third-class bar.

Général de la Chanterelle was known to every policeman in Boulogne as being a man of integrity and a personal friend of *Monsieur le Commissaire*. No objection had therefore been raised when he requested that he be allowed to station himself at the foot of the gangway. He leaned on his silver-topped stick, his one sound eye fixed unblinkingly on the exit from the Customs Hall.

"Funny thing," said the Purser meditatively to the Chief Steward, "how things have changed. I remember these day-trips before the war, when the police used to wheel the drunks aboard in hand-carts. Fighting, they used to be. And now look at 'em. Mild as a bunch of schoolgirls."

"True, Cyril, true. Proper dull it is nowadays. You don't need a master-at-arms. You need an arithmetic mistress. I wonder who the old boy in the black eyeglass is waiting for."

His curiosity was satisfied within a matter of seconds. As Trevor Hilgrove came out of the Customs Hall, the General took a step forward. Trevor stopped as if he had been turned to stone. For the second time Nemesis, in a tussore suit, a panama hat and a black eyeglass, was waiting, and in a transparent moment of time, he knew that unless he could placate his enemy, during the next five seconds, disaster, utter and irrevocable, was upon him. Once up the gangway and aboard ship, he would be all right—and only then. Fifteen feet of quay lay between him and sanctuary. He advanced cautiously, every muscle braced. The General twirled his stick and his moustache.

"Trouble brewing, George?" said the Purser eagerly.

"Unless I'm very greatly mistaken, you are correct, Cyril."

Confronted by the General, Trevor stopped. He managed a weak but winning smile. He said politely:

"Excuse me, Sir. You are in the way. I want to go on board, please."

The General whipped a dirty visiting-card from his pocket and thrust it under Trevor's nose.

"Is this your card?"

"My card?" He read swiftly:

MAURICE SEVRIER.	
Taxis:	All Informations:
English Spokken.	Specialities.

Ah! This was a way out. He said easily:

"That, Sir, is *not* my card. I am a British subject, my name is Trevor Hilgrove, and I demand that you let me pass. If you do not do so, I shall complain to the British Consul."

"If this is not your card—and I know that it is not—permit me to tell you that you are a liar, a liar and a vagabond." He raised his stick. Trevor hurriedly put his dart-board on the quay and backed away a step, his hands up and his fists clenched. The General's lip curled.

"A liar, a vagabond—and a coward. I only set myself into conflict with brave men."

He turned and, with a contemptuous flick of his stick, sent the dart-board rolling. Trevor Hilgrove gave a strangled, agonised shout.

As if impelled by its own malicious sense of direction, the dart-board trundled towards the edge of the quay, appeared to hesitate coquettishly on the brink, spun slowly round once —and plunged into thirty feet of water, mud and sludge.

A few bubbles wavered to the surface and burst with a gurgling sound among the scum and the orange-peel of Boulogne harbour.

CHAPTER TWENTY-TWO

Jim Carver walked alone. He had waited until the very last moment outside that café place, and now there was a bare five minutes, no six, before the boat would sail. It wasn't much time in which a man could make or break his life. He crossed the bridge, that same bridge that he had walked only this very morning on his way to look for George Holden, before he had ever known or cared whether the little Normandy girl in the pinafore was alive or dead. If he had bothered to think at all about this young singer of old songs on a sunny morning, he wouldn't have remembered her as a living person, but as a pair of sunburned hands making butter and as the source of a song. The song had been remembered and more acutely felt because it had come to him during a brief respite from the clatter and the dirt of war. He only realised now, years after, how blessed those days in a Normandy orchard had been, and how the simple fact of being physically clean and of being able to wash the separator in the dairy had calmed him and restored him and healed him. He had found strength and sanity in the smooth handle of a spade, in the sight of corn curtsying after the stroke of the sickle. It was queer, the sense of continuity you got from things like that. Even as a boy he never remembered learning how to work the land. No one had ever told him that a cow was nigh on calving when her strings slackened. You knew, not by a book, but by the texture of the sky and by the smell of the wind, the right moment to put a field under plough. What civil servant knew or could confirm that the right thing to do was to put cobwebs on a cut or that old ale—or better still draught cider mixed with treacle was a fine stimulant for calves. You knew these things immemorially, and when you got away from them, they pulled you back.

He'd got away from them when a Cotswold farmer became a Lancer. But they'd come back. George Holden had brought them back, with his talk of clover mixtures for grazing leys and breeding to bloodlines and parsnips for butter fat, speaking of fields that he'd never seen and never would see now. Then, when George was killed, there didn't seem to be much point. The call had come again in Normandy, but it had only been a brief summons then, for the German armies were breaking, the hunt was up and the Lancers were harking forrard. France, the Ardennes, the Rhine, Hamburg, Lubeck and the Baltic—and then Dover, the Depot, demob. He'd been restless, he supposed, after going so far and seeing so much, and that's why he'd stayed in London, shutting his ears to what he knew in his heart to be the slow, sure pulse of his blood.

In Marie-Josephe the sound had become articulate. In the work of her hands he had seen clearly the work which his own hands were shaped to do. She had pointed the way and shown him, if ever a woman had shown a man anything, that it was a path that she would gladly tread at his side. All these schemes that he'd worked out with George could have come true. They could have been real and shared with a woman he loved. God Almighty, it was even funny, in a way, how George and he, a couple of unmarried sergeants, had solemnly thought up a plan to interest other people's children in the land. Other people's children! With Marie-Josephe to bear them, he could guide his own sons' hands to the plough. It was a thought that lifted his heart and straightened his back. And what was it that Luke Grenfell had said? He had asked Jim what he was looking for. He knew now. It was a constant and abiding Love, rooted in the life for which he had been born.

"Par ici, Monsieur."

"Thank you."

He entered the narrow passage, dim after the sunshine outside, and showed his passport at the window. As the official stamped it and slid a boarding-card inside, he asked Jim how much French money he was taking out of France. Only the same amount that he'd brought in—less the price of a bottle of wine. "Monsieur has not had an expensive day." "No, I suppose not." He went on into the Customs Hall. No. He had nothing to declare. He had bought nothing, no presents for anybody, nothing at all. The Customs Official said with a smile, "Next time you come to France, you must stay longer, Monsieur. *Au revoir."*

"Au revoir."

Well, that was the last of France, definitely the last. He walked slowly across the cobbles towards the gangway. Something had obviously happened, for half a dozen porters were gazing over the side of the quay into the water, shrugging and gesticulating, and a fierce old gentleman was being pacified by two policemen. Jim glanced up towards the ship. He saw Trevor Hilgrove's face, white and contorted with fury, looking over the rail. Charley Brewer was there too, rubbing his cheek as if someone had slapped him—and Luke Grenfell—and Mr. Collins—all standing in a group, staring at the scummy surface of the sea.

"Hurry up, please."

"Yes. Sorry."

Jim handed over his boarding ticket. He hesitated for a moment, wanting still to feel the soil of France under his feet. Then he walked with deliberation up the gangway and along the deck. Through the window of the first-class saloon he saw Mr. Hetherington, Mr. Thomson, Mr. Johnson and Mr. Pratt sitting around a table. Mr. Hetherington was dealing. Jim walked on aft. He said to Luke Grenfell:

"What's up?"

"I'll tell you later. Did your Marie-Josephe turn up?"

"No."

He moved a step away from the others and leaned on the rail. The gangway was lowered and dragged on its rollers across the cobbles. The ropes that bound the vessel fore and aft to the quay were cast off, splashed into the water. A man slow to anger, he was aware of an upsurging of resentment. It was an impersonal, cold rage, directed against the bricks and stones of Boulogne. Somebody spoke to him and he said, "Oh, go to hell." With narrowed eyes and taut muscles he stood looking at France. Then, suddenly, he saw what he wanted to see more than anything in the world.

Despite her determination neither to see nor to be seen, Marie-Josephe was unable to restrain herself from standing up and walking to the window of the buffet. She had driven the General at breakneck speed from the ramparts to the harbour and had then slipped away to sit in a corner in solitary unhappiness and self-reproach. She wanted the vessel to leave quickly now, and yet she wanted it to stay. She drew the curtain back a very little and looked. Almost imperceptibly, the vast bulk leaned away from the shore and her heart sank. It was quite safe to come out now and she wanted passionately to be away from this place and alone.

She walked slowly out of the buffet and into the evening

sunshine. There was her car. She opened the door and got into it and pressed the self-starter. Nothing happened, nothing at all. It occurred to her how utterly lost and helpless she was without the man whom the cruel ship was taking away from her for ever. At that moment, she heard a shout. . . .

When Jim saw Marie-Josephe walking to her car, he acted instinctively. Before he knew what he was doing, he had climbed over the rail. With a lightning glance he measured the ever-widening distance between ship and shore. He shook off the hand that clutched his shoulder. The propellers were kicking up a smother of foam, churning the harbour as he leapt. His feet touched the edge of the quay and slipped. Desperately he clutched at a rusted ring, hung suspended for a fearful moment, drew himself strongly upwards. Policemen and porters were running towards him and the old gentleman in the tussore suit was waving his stick. He evaded them with ease. Laughing, he jumped the wooden barrier. He saw Marie-Josephe leave her car and come towards him. Never had he seen a woman's face so radiant.

So, to the shrilling of police-whistles and the shouting of men, a Lancer came back to France.

Savez-vous planter les choux?

Savez-vous planter les choux?